TEACHING STUDENTS TO WRITE

A GUIDE TO TEACHING THIRD THROUGH NINTH GRADERS ALL ASPECTS OF WRITING

BY SCOTT PURDY

Also by Scott Purdy

Time Management for Teachers
Tomorrow Begins at 3:00
The Write Time Teacher Planbook
A Hands On Approach to Teaching Statistics, Probability, and Graphing
A Hands On Approach to Teaching Measurement
A Hands On Approach to Teaching Logic
A Hands On Approach to Teaching Geometry
A Hands On Approach to Teaching Algebra
A Hands On Approach to Teaching Patterns and Functions
A Hands On Approach to Teaching Number and Operations

For information, please contact
WRITE TIME PUBLISHING
2121 Rebild Dr. Solvang, California 93463-2217
(800) 824-3376
FAX: (805) 688-7802
online: www.writetimepub.com

Table of Contents

Setting the Goal

Through experience, I have developed some different approaches to the way in which an effective writing program should be structured. The typical method is to assess the existing level of students and then move forward from that point. While it is important to identify the ability of individual students, it is not the key to creating successful writers.

The first step in organizing your writing program is to establish the ultimate goal of the writers in your class. What should the typical fourth, or fifth, or eighth grade paper look like at the end of the school year? What is a reasonable and attainable level of success for your grade? What should your average student be able to write, and what should the variation be between the low-end, average, and high-end student's paper?

If we do not establish the fundamental goal of where we want our writers to be, we will never be able to accurately measure their level of success. We often be-

1

come so mired in teaching isolated skills of how to punctuate, capitalize, structure sentences, and enrich vocabulary that we never get to the end product.

When primary teachers teach young students to read, there are letter sounds to teach, blends, dipthongs and the general phonetic rules. These sounds become words which eventually become phrases, and the phrases become sentences. With practice, the sentences become paragraphs. Since this is the fundamental way we teach reading, it would follow that teaching writing should be the same.

Teaching writing is not like teaching reading. Students do not learn to write from the word to the phrase to the sentence to the paragraph to the story; they must learn from the multi-paragraph essay or story and work back through the basic components. The primary goal of their practice should not focus on writing individual sentences or paragraphs; rather, they need practice from the start at writing lengthy compositions. For third graders, this translates to three and four paragraph essays or reports and multi-page stories. For ninth graders this means multi-paragraph essays with well-developed introductions and conclusions and stories with plot, theme, and character development. Writing is based on whole thoughts and schemes.

I believe the main reason students complete the first paragraph of an assignment and then say, "That's all I can think of," is that we have taught them, since the second grade, that a paragraph is a complete thought. A paragraph is an "isolated" thought that needs connection to other paragraphs in order to be complete.

When we begin to teach students to start thinking in terms of multiple reasons why, different approaches to, and various possible outcomes, we are beginning the mental organizational process which enables students to become effective writers. It is at this point that they begin thinking about two or three (or more) approaches, angles, or outcomes. From this, they learn to support and give examples, and this is what writing is all about.

My students can't even put a sentence together. How do you expect them to write multiple paragraph essays or stories?

We have to look at the big picture. When students write sentences, they are not thinking the same way that they do when they write essays. We must start the training early to have them think in these big "chunks." For example, how often have you had your students write a story and watch as they immediately put pencil to paper and start writing. They do not plan, and they do not know where the story is going. At the beginning of each school year, I receive papers that are rambling, point-less, and impossible to correct because the entire concept of what they have written is fundamentally flawed.

If we ask our students to write about why they like hats, we want to train them from the start to think of multiple reasons. When students begin thinking in this way, the overall cohesion of the writing, the paragraph organization, and the purpose of the paper is clear from the start. With a unified whole, the teacher can begin to refine the parts.

I would much prefer to get an organized essay or story with horrible mechanics and weak wordings than a mechanically correct, thesaurus-filled composition which had absolutely no organizational structure. In the latter, there is no foundation — there is nothing to save.

When you write a letter, do you first worry about mechanics and sentence structure or the concept of what you're going to say? This is how we must teach our students to approach their writing.

In this long answer to the original question, your kids may have great difficulty putting sentences together, but they can organize their thoughts. This will give them a purpose to learn the mechanics and other skills they need to complete a writing assignment. Think of the process of writing as if it were a house. Until there is a vision of how the finished product will look, learning to nail, wire, plumb, paint, and cut are random skills — important, but leading nowhere on their own.

If my students write three (or five) paragraph reports, the mechanics (spelling, punctuation, capitalization, usage) will be atrocious. Do you expect me to spend days correcting them?

I wish I could say, "Oh, don't worry, correcting is easy!" I'm a writing teacher, and I know how long it takes to correct papers. I spend many long hours on this tedious task. There are numerous ways to ease or simplify this burden which I share in the closing chapter. One aspect of correcting that you need keep in the back of your mind is that you are a teacher, not an editor. A second consideration is that students can be easily overwhelmed by your corrections.

Think back to the fundamental question of this chapter: "What do you want your students to be able to write at the end of this school year?" They are not going to accomplish this in one assignment. For each student we need to have a plan, or hierarchy, of how they will attain a desired level. If a student cannot write neatly, cannot spell, cannot correctly punctuate sentences, cannot remember to indent paragraphs, uses weak vocabulary, and is three days late in handing in his or her paper, he or she faces some major hurdles. Our job is to help him or her get over one hurdle at a time. When we correct a paper with so many flaws, it is like stacking all of the hurdles on top of one another. The student will run into them or walk away without hope.

How long does it take to correct these papers?

The task becomes manageable when you begin to correct what the student can handle. In the case given above, I would look at sentences and neatness — only. The goal on the rewrite of that paper or the next paper written by that student is to be absolutely certain that sentence structure and neatness are improved. Once you have focused the student, he now has a manageable and measurable task.

Identifying this hierarchy of skills and enabling all teachers to pinpoint the priorities of what any individual student needs to improve upon is the purpose of this book.

What is the point of having my students write pages of a story that goes on and on when the first paragraph alone is 200 words and has no periods?

I have already answered half of this question; but basically, students are going to learn writing in a very different way. When we approach something differently, it takes time to do it well. Your third or fourth graders will have great difficulty with this "whole story" concept, but if we do not get them started in these early grades, then fifth and sixth graders will have the same amount of difficulty when it is first presented to them.

I am thoroughly convinced that the reason high school students struggle so much with writing is that they simply have never had sufficient practice to master this whole paper approach. They are still practicing the habit of connecting one sentence to the next, rather than analyzing the whole paper.

We must teach this essential skill as early as possible, and then provide practice at mastering specifics at grade-appropriate levels.

Is this one of those writing programs that is so concerned about harming the child's creativity (inner self) that everything and anything they write is acceptable?

6

Nothing could be further from the truth. As a classroom teacher, I am the most fussy, meticulous, and demanding person you will ever meet; yet, at the same time, I am probably as relaxed and fun-loving with my students as any teacher you will find. Since I clearly know my desired outcome and have identified the steps to get there, the pressure is off, and I can enjoy my job.

Every student must learn to punctuate properly, to spell well or to find a method to eliminate spelling errors, to know and apply capitalization rules, to select and use sophisticated vocabulary, to write neatly or type, to organize paragraphs properly, to vary sentence length and structure, and to be responsible to turn in work on time.

At each grade level a student can attain a level of success. When students do reach this proficiency, there is no need to create a false sense of self-worth by accepting or praising mediocrity. Students who know "they can" develop a sense of "inner praise." I know this is true because I see it in my students' eyes each year. My experience is that the closer they get to grade level mastery, the more confident and creative they become.

We still must create the "goal paper," but before we discuss that, we need to establish ground level or as I prefer to call it, the bottom of the quicksand.

If we are going to adopt this "whole paper" approach, students must be able to spell basic words and at least understand the concept that words come together to make sentences. A sentence explains a basic thought. Typically, most students achieve this basic understanding somewhere between the end of first and the middle of third grade. Of course, there are exceptions.

Students must have knowledge of general penmanship and the organization of paragraphs. They need not necessarily know that a paragraph reflects a unified thought, but they must know the concept that paragraphs divide a longer bit of writing into "subgroups."

Understanding what a sentence is and that a paragraph is a part of a whole are pretty basic concepts. Most third or fourth graders know this and are therefore ready to begin writing. Do not assume that since they cannot write in complete sentences, cannot spell all the words they are writing, and do not have a rich vocabulary that they cannot begin a writing program. They are ready.

How does one go about creating an end product or goal?

As an eighth grade writing teacher for many years, I have a clear concept in my mind as to how a quality paper, written by a fourteen year old, should look. It is not enough, however, to simply know it when I see it; I need to describe it, to put it into words, and to break it down into fundamental parts. It almost becomes a formula. The more clear I am in my mind of the component parts, the better I will be at explaining this to my students. The following is a list of ingredients:

The organizational structure

1. The paper should be of multiple-paragraph length, preferably four or more paragraphs, with a clear opening and closing paragraph.

2. The opening paragraph must begin with at least three sentences which create interest or intrigue for the reader. There are a number of ways to accomplish this.

3. The last (or second to the last) sentences of the opening paragraph must introduce the topic of the essay (as in a thesis) but must not give any information about the topic. The topic(s) should simply be stated within one sentence.

4. Body paragraphs must be of similar length and develop different aspects of the thesis. They must give at least one or two supporting examples.

5. The closing paragraph must link or connect to either the title or the way in which interest was created in the opening paragraph. The thesis or purpose must be restated in different words, and there must be a "twist" or final statement which causes the reader to either nod with agreement or smile.

6. A clever or thought-provoking title should be included.

The internal structure

1. Sentences within each paragraph must switch between simple, compound, and complex sentences.

2. No two sentences may begin the same way within one paragraph, and at least two sentences in each paragraph should begin with a transition word or phrase.
3. No two paragraphs may begin with the same word or phrase.
4. The word "and" must not appear more than once in any sentence.
5. Each body paragraph should end with a sentence which brings the topic to a natural close. Transition statements between paragraphs must start, but never end a preceding paragraph.
6. There should be a transitional sentence or two between the opening three sentences of interest and the thesis or purpose statement.

Vocabulary

1. Highly descriptive adjectives, adverbs or verbs should not be repeated within a paragraph.
2. Each sentence should contain a blend of single and multi-syllable words.
3. Vocabulary should stretch for the perfect word but should not over-stretch (Thesaurusitis).
4. Verb tense should be consistently past tense.

Mechanics

1. Spelling, punctuation, usage, and capitalization should be near perfect with no more than three to five mechanics errors in the entire paper.

Personal traits

1. The interest in the opening, the examples in the body, and the twist at the end should be creative and unique to the writer.
2. The arguments and conviction of the paper must show depth, sophistication, or thought. The writer must avoid a superficial presentation.
3. The entire essay must be unified around the theme of the thesis.

Basic omissions

1. Avoid slang.
2. Never refer to your essay (in this paragraph, etc.).

There are probably some requirements which may have raised some eyebrows. Please keep in mind that this is my criteria for my eighth graders in my classroom. It is not a recommendation for every eighth grade teacher. We must each decide the level of expectation for the children with whom we work.

Realistically, unless a teacher has many years of experience teaching writing, the development of the "goal paper" is a challenging process. I am not suggesting that you attempt to create your goals at this point. As the chapters unfold, continue to make mental notes, and by the time all the information is presented, I believe you will be ready to define your own "goal paper."

My approach to teaching writing ascribes to the philosophy that structure creates freedom. I believe that when students understand the structure, parameters, and formula of a complete essay or composition, they can blossom as creative writers.

In my class, I compare a good writer to a good artist. Anyone can put a brush to a canvas, but until an artist learns to mix and blend color, masters brush strokes, uses light, understands the mathematics of proportion, knows the secret of what must be painted first, and knows when to stop painting, he or she will never be a complete or accomplished artist.

There is a hierarchy of skills in art and writing. The sooner a student learns to work within this hierarchy, the more accomplished his or her writing will be.

Superficial vs. Personal
and
Creative vs. Expository

We must find a way to make some sense out of how writing assignments are categorized. I have seen many curriculum guides which differentiate student writing into categories or domains. Each one that I read seems logical but also seems to "muddy the water" in terms of all that you are supposed to do as a teacher. If it is confusing to you, imagine the frustration of your students.

They are trying to figure out clever ways to write "transitions" and "clincher sentences" which they hear are integral parts of the structure, but the teacher keeps changing the rules: "Oh no, this is a narrative, therefore..." or, "OK, students, remember that when you write a story, the paragraphs don't need...". I believe we need to simplify the approach for you and your students.

Let us begin with the following example of delineations or domains of types of writing:

- Story
- Autobiographical incident
- Biography
- Report of information
- Observational writing
- Reflection
- Problem & Solution
- Evaluation
- Speculation about cause and effect
- Controversial issue
- Interpretation

This is one sample of many such categorizations which are presented in writing texts and curriculum guides. From an awareness standpoint, this type of listing is very useful. I would be the first to agree that through a student's career in school, he or she needs experience and practice writing in each of these domains. However, I am not convinced that writing, from the viewpoint of the student, should be this compartmentalized. The teacher needs to keep this type of organizational structure in the background to be referred to as we do our year-long planning.

Typically, we also classify writing into three basic approaches: creative writing, descriptive writing, and expository writing. We then try to figure out a way to blend all of this together and often get frustrated and say, "I won't have enough time to correct it, and my students don't write well enough to do justice to all of this anyway; therefore, I will do what I have always done — a book report here, a story there, some poetry on the side, and voilà, writing!"

You are reading this book because you want to do more than that. I assure you, there is nothing magical about the process. We can do it all.

First, I believe any assignment can be creative, and I believe that any assignment can be expository. Additionally, I believe every assignment should be descriptive. The depth of the "creativity" and "exposition" are based upon whether the assignment itself is superficial or personal.

Let me first try to explain the terms and give a couple of examples. Remember, the goal here is to simplify the ways in which we teach children how to write.

Creative vs. Expository

I constantly hear parents express the concern, "I wish my daughter/son had time to do more creative writing. She/ he loves to write, but all of the assignments seem so dull." I then hear fellow teachers respond, "I wish I had time to do more creative writing, but students are going to have to do expository writing in high school and college. They need to learn the structure."

I simply do not buy into the concept that creative means freedom and fun, and expository means structure and drudgery. Any of the writing domains presented on the previous page can be both creative and expository.

Creative writing simply means that the student uses the imagination to create. Expository means that the student is attempting to "expose" or present information to the reader. I do not see a dichotomy here.

Superficial vs. Personal

The term "superficial" sounds derogatory. That is not the intent. Superficial is my word to describe assignments that do not require deep thought on the part of the student. The value of these assignments is that they are a quick check on the students' mastery of mechanics, organization, and speed. Students will have to do this type of writing on essay tests and in-class assignments many times in the future. They need to learn to do superficial writing. Most letters that we write are superficial (as adults, that is most of the writing we do).

As teachers, we assign a lot of superficial writing. Here are some examples of superficial assignments:

What are three ways in which your friends are beneficial to you?

Tell what you liked and disliked about the book you read.

How were the characters _____ and _____ similar, and why do you think the author presented them in this way?

Most of us have given assignments similar to these examples, and there is nothing wrong with them. They are simply superficial in terms of having students use their imaginations or apply their personal experience.

"Personal" writing is structured in precisely the same way as superficial writing except that it takes more time and thought. In personal writing, the student must include or emphasize his or her background, values, or experience. Students cannot do personal writing in a forty-five minute class period, but any assignment can be restructured to become personal.

The three examples of superficial assignments could be altered as follows to become personal:

"What are three ways in which your friends are beneficial to you?" might become: In your life, you have developed friendships with adults, siblings, classmates, and relatives. These "friends" have undoubtedly changed your life in many ways. You may not realize it, but your friendships with these people have changed their lives as well. Select one or two people who you believe have been affected in either a positive or negative way by your friendship. Give examples of why you believe you have had this impact.

"Tell what you liked and disliked about the book you read." would change to: Someone once said, "The perfect book has never been written." Basically this means that in every book we read, there are some sections we appreciate more than others. In the book you just finished, select either your favorite section or your least favorite section and compare how it is similar to something that has happened to you, personally. If you select a section that you disliked, explain how it was unrealistic as compared to your experience. Regardless of the approach you choose, write one paragraph which explains what happened in the book, a second paragraph that explains what happened to you, and a third paragraph which compares the similarities.

"How were the characters ____ and ____ similar and why do you think the author presented them in this way?" could change to: ____ and ____ were two of the dominant characters in the book. With which of them did you most readily identify and why? You might develop aspects of how your personalities, physical traits, or reactions to situations are similar. In addition, discuss why you did not identify as closely with the other character. You may write your response as a combination of the two characters if you find yourself to be a blend. For example, you might share specific personality traits with one and share other traits with the other.

It obviously takes more explanation to reach into the thoughts of the students. You will also find that you spend more class time explaining the assignment and reading sample paragraphs students have written. The sample assignments described in a later chapter attempt to reach for a more personal reaction.

You might think of this superficial versus personal writing on a scale. Different assignments will (and should) fall in various locations on the line.

Superficial   Personal
|———|

The benefit of this simplification is that when we remove the mystique and jargon of the domains and simplify this into a matter of deciding whether an assignment is superficial or personal, we can teach the structure of every writing assignment in the same way. The student need not worry about writing a cause and effect essay one way, a problem/solution paper another, and a story a third way.

This is where our creativity must come forth. If student writing is going to be interesting, thought-provoking, and challenging, we need to be more creative in the assignments we give.

As teachers, we must be aware of the domains of writing, but our students need not be bogged down in terminology. We have to give them a basic structure and then stand back and let them be creative. The more assignments we can provide which allow them to put themselves into the content, the more creative they will be. Creative writing, expository writing, descriptive writing and story writing can all be taught with the same structure and the same terminology.

The Year-long Writing Plan

In the preceding chapter, I described how I judge the sophistication of essay topics. As a self-contained teacher in elementary school or a departmentalized teacher with six different classes per day, one of your first tasks each year should be to devise your year-long writing plan.

The preliminary step is to list the topics, units, or novels (genre) to be covered. We then place this information on a chart to find connections between content areas. Taking into account our district's writing requirements, report card and conferencing schedule, school vacations, and personal considerations, we schedule how writing assignments will integrate into a year-long calendar. It is a very straightforward process and once completed will save many hours of planning time during the school year.

It is not my intent to describe how a self-contained teacher would organize the instruction in social studies and science. I group these into what I call the "content" areas. I am also not going to include math in the mix. One of my other books, Tomorrow Begins at 3:00, suggests an approach to year-long planning which incorporates all subject areas. In this chapter, I limit the discussion to listing the content units and then describe how I would feature these to develop a writing program.

Imagine that you are a sixth grade teacher preparing for a new school year. You know what novels you will read as a class, and are aware of the science and social studies units you will present. You have decided that students should read a library book each month of the school year, but there are also four novels that you will read as a class. There is, of course, basic reading instruction as well. Given this information, you are ready to prepare your year-long writing plan.

Your district requires (or you decide) that your students must complete writing assignments in the following categories: report of information, letter writing, biography, autobiography, story, explaining a process, and observational writing.

If you are like most teachers, you look at this requirement and wonder when you are supposed to do all of this and still teach content areas, reading, and math.

As a self-contained teacher, make a commitment that all writing assignments will link to other curricular areas. There will be no writing for writing's sake. All of the students' work will focus upon a curricular purpose.

Second, every student is going to do two writing assignments per month — approximately one every two weeks. Over the year, if we deduct the close of school, odd vaca-

22

tion weeks, etc., you will assign about sixteen papers — probably more than you have ever required. Keep in mind, however, that these writing assignments will probably fill between sixty and one hundred nights of homework.

The Year-long Plan: Step 1

We start this process by outlining the units, chapters, and number of pages to be covered in content areas.

Sixth Grade Science Book

Unit 1 - Ecosystems
      Chapter 1: Organisms and Relationships (12 pages)
      Chapter 2: The Food Chain (12)
      Chapter 3: Ecosystems (19)
Unit 2 - Botany
      Chapter 4: Leaf Structure (13)
      Chapter 5: Storage and Transport in Plants (15)
Unit 3 - Physiology/Anatomy
      Chapter 6: The Skeletal System (12)
      Chapter 7: The Digestive and Excretory Systems (11)
      Chapter 8: The Respiratory and Circulatory Systems (20)
Unit 4 - Physiology/Anatomy
      Chapter 9: The Nervous System (17)
      Chapter 10: The Life Cycle (15)
      Chapter 11: Health and Physical Fitness (19)
Unit 5 - Energy/Physical Science
      Chapter 12: Work and Energy (13)
      Chapter 13: Electricity (15)
      Chapter 14: Magnetism (19)

Unit 6 - Physics
        Chapter 15: Today's Energy Sources (15)
        Chapter 16: Tomorrow's Energy Sources (19)
Unit 7 - Ecology
        Chapter 17: Water on Planet Earth (15)
        Chapter 18: The Oceans (15)
        Chapter 19: Resources from Water (21)
Unit 8 - Astronomy
        Chapter 20: The Stars (15)
        Chapter 21: Mysteries of the Universe (13)
        Chapter 22: Space Travel (19)

Total pages: 344
Vocabulary words per unit: approximately 12

You must decide if it is possible to cover the entire book. With thirty-eight weeks in the school year, less one week at the beginning of and another non-content week at the close, you will need to complete eight units in thirty-six weeks. This allows about four and one-half weeks per unit. Therefore, it is probably possible to cover all of the material. Longer units could be given five or six weeks, shorter or less interesting units could take three or four weeks.

Sixth Grade Social Studies

Unit 1 - The Past and Present World
        Chapter 1: People of the World (12)
        Chapter 2: Places (20)
        Chapter 3: Learning about the Past (24)
Unit 2 - The Earliest People
        Chapter 4: Understanding Time (16)
        Chapter 5: How Societies Developed (15)

Unit 3 - Middle Eastern Civilizations
        Chapter 6:   Mesopotamia (25)
        Chapter 7:   Ancient Egypt (24)
Unit 4 - Early Asian Civilizations
        Chapter 8:   India (22)
        Chapter 9:   China (19)
Unit 5 - Beginnings of Western Ideas
        Chapter 10:   The Israelites (17)
        Chapter 11:   Ancient Greece (23)
        Chapter 12:   Classical Greece (21)
Unit 6 - Rome
        Chapter 13:   Beginning of Roman Civilization (24)
        Chapter 14:   The Roman Empire (17)
        Chapter 15:   The Fall of Rome (17)

Total pages: 296
Vocabulary words per unit: approximately 12

Again, you must decide if you can cover all units. Given thirty-six teaching weeks, you will have six weeks to present each unit.

I must add a personal bias at this point and emphasize the importance of presenting the complete science and social studies curricula. It is so easy to give in and only present four or five of the units in content area books. Insufficient time, constant interruptions, and the educational buzzwords that, "less is more," all tempt one to cut out the "less meaningful" chapters. When, however, will children discover new areas of interest if we do not give them all of the experiences? The commitment for a year-long plan forces or enables us to present the complete curriculum.

The Year-long Plan: Step 2

How long will you spend on each content area unit? Should you present information in the order it appears in the book, or would it make sense to alter the order to align units? It is a challenge to answer these questions so I suggest you create a chart as shown on pages 28 and 29.

Plan around vacations, conferences, grading, etc. In the given plan, I have not altered the order of presentation, but I did decide that I wanted to spend longer on the Greek and Roman Civilizations unit. I shortened the unit on India because there are not as many resources to enhance my teaching. I also decided not to correct papers during winter or spring vacations. Therefore, my writing assignments will be due the week prior to vacations so I can correct and return them before these school holidays begin.

Another aspect of this planning is that for every two weeks (ten school days), I will plan only eight daily lessons. Realistically, I will lose one day every two weeks to an unforeseen scheduling problem. With my tendency to overplan, I have built in one extra day to complete my objectives. In my experience, should I actually have ten days of teaching, it is much easier to add something new than to leave out something for which I have already prepared.

On the charts on pages 28 and 29, I included novels we will read as a class. I want to try to blend these into my content areas to avoid feeling compelled to have my students write a book synopsis in addition to their other writing assignments. Sixteen extended writing assignments are sufficient.

The Year-long Plan: Step 3

The sets of writing assignments presented in the writing column of the year-long planning charts are described more completely in the Sample Assignments chapter. For clarification, I will progress through the year with a brief explanation of each suggested topic. The curriculum outlined below is not a proposed sixth grade program; rather, it is a model to help teachers envision how a year-long plan might be structured.

Essay Set 1: Autobiography (presented on page 188)

Since the school year typically begins with a variety of opening of school activities, I suggest beginning the year with an autobiographical essay. This will provide an opportunity to learn more about the individuals in your classroom.

The second essay in this set is another autobiography, but in this case, it might be entitled, "It's a Bug's Life." Students switch their point of view and write as though they are an animal somewhere in the food chain. The animal must create an autobiographical story about the victories, the trials, and the tribulations of its role in nature's "survival of the fittest." Students will apply information learned in Unit 1 of their science book, and there is a definite link to the concept being studied in social studies as well.

	Science	Social Studies	Literature	Writing
Week 1				**Autobiography** Self
Week 2	**Unit 1** Ecosystems & Food Chain	**Unit 1** Past and Present World		
Week 3				**Autobiography** Animal in Food Chain
Week 4				
Week 5				**Legend** Early people explaining nature
Week 6	**Unit 2** Botany		**Novel**	
Week 7	Leaves & Transportation		Biography	**Legend** Refuting myths based upon fact
Week 8		**Unit 2** Earliest People		
Week 9				**Observational Essay** Plants
Week 10				
Week 11	**Unit 3** Physiology Body Systems			**Observational Essay**
Week 12		**Unit 3** Mesopotamia		Character Sketch of Earliest People
Week 13				
Week 14		Egypt	**Novel** The Egypt Game	**Letter Writing** business letter
Week 15				
Week 16	**Unit 4** Physiology Body Sytems & Health			**Letter Writing Book Report** friendly letter
Week 17				
Week 18		**Unit 4** India		**Step-by-step Process** Body system
Week 19				

	Science	Social Studies	Literature	Writing
Week 20	**Unit 5** Energy	China		**Step-by-step** **Process** in reverse
Week 21				
Week 22				
Week 23				**Comparison** **Essay**
Week 24		**Unit 5** Israel		India-China
Week 25	**Unit 6** Physics			**Contrast** **Essay**
Week 26		Greek Civilization	**Novel** A Collection	Energy
Week 27			of Ancient	**Myth** Greek or
Week 28			Mythology	Roman
Week 29	**Unit 7** Water			**Myth** Present day
Week 30	Resources			treatment
Week 31		**Unit 6** Roman		**Time Machine** **Travel**
Week 32		Civilization	**Novel** Science	
Week 33	**Unit 8** Astronomy		Fiction	**Futuristic** **Essay**
Week 34		Roman Empire		Looking back on life
Week 35				
Week 36		Fall of Rome		
Week 37				
Week 38				

Essay Set 2: Myth or Legend (presented on page 220)

Both of these assignments are clearly explained in the Sample Assignments chapter. The content link here is that students will complete their first social studies unit on the "Past and Present World" and begin the "Earliest People" unit. Writing a legend provides great freedom for students and will allow those who are intrigued with story writing to shine. Obviously, early people created their own legends to explain the forces of nature.

The second essay allows the analytical mind to take over. In this essay, students will exchange legend papers and scientifically refute the logic or credibility of a classmate's paper. This introduces the scientific method into the curriculum while demonstrating a fundamental difference between our ancestors and us — education, knowledge, and technology.

Essay Set 3: Observational Essay (presented on page 199)

These essays are typically classified as "descriptive writing." While they are not listed together as a set in the Sample Assignments chapter, they will work well as described here.

In the first essay, linking to the botany unit, students will need to present a thorough description of the physical appearance of a leaf or some other organic material. The writer should seek to make this a sensory description in which sight, touch, smell, sound, and possibly taste are paragraph topics.

The second essay is a physical description of a person the student has never met. In this case, the person will be of the same tribe or clan in a primitive society (as described in the social studies book). The student must provide a complete physical description of this imaginary friend and must also describe his or her personality.

Essay Set 4: Letter Writing (described on page 212)

A review of the structure of a friendly letter and business letter is a yearly task for fourth through ninth graders. A letter can and should be written in the same format as any extended essay. Letters need introductions, thesis statements, body paragraphs and closings. In the first of these two assignments, students will write a letter to Gilgamesh, Sargon of Akkad, Shamshi-Adad, Hammurabi, or Nebuchadnezzar registering a complaint or paying a compliment about his treatment as their ruler.

The second assignment will be a friendly letter to one of the characters in the novel, The Egypt Game.

Essay Set 5: Step-by-step Process (presented on page 226)

As students continue their study of the body's sytems in science, an explanation of how or why one of the body's functions works is a natural link. Topics such as why people sneeze, cough, hiccup, bleed, have heart attacks, etc. provide a wonderful application of learned knowledge.

The second essay takes a different approach to explaining a step-by-step process in that students must begin with an existing condition and describe how this came to be. In other words, the process is reversed. Since students have completed their studies of Mesopotamia and Egypt, they might select one of the fundamental advancements or achievements by one of these societies. For example:

The pyramids could not have been built if the Egyptians had not developed sophisticated mathematical processes, the technology of how to cut and shape stone, and the ability to transport stone over great distance.

The Code of Hammurabi would never have survived without the development of a system of writing, the ability to etch these letters into stone, and the development of bronze as a means of making tools and weapons.

The teacher might want to broaden the scope for this assignment from merely the histories already presented to include achievements from other civilizations (Greeks or Romans). This might provide a means of foreshadowing or introducing future societies to be discussed in social studies.

Essay Set 6: Comparison and Contrast

These essays are very straight-forward in that they are both four or five paragraphs in length and describe either two or three similarities or differences between two items.

In the first, students will either compare (telling similarities between) Indian and Chinese civilizations or contrast (explaining differences between) Indian and Chinese civilizations.

In the second, students will shift their analysis to the science unit on energy. In this case, they will either compare or contrast different aspects of energy. For example: kinetic versus potential energy, alternating versus direct current, force versus work, magnetism versus electromagnetism, or electricity versus magnetism.

Essay Set 7: Myths (presented on page 220)

We would miss a wonderful teaching opportunity if, when studying the Greeks and Romans, we did not have students write a myth. Earlier in the year they wrote a legend, and we can use that experience to enhance this assignment.

The second essay in this set will have students update a myth from their in-class reading to a present day setting. The characters and the location will be current, but the theme will remain ancient. For example, "Theseus and the Minotaur" might become "Billy and the Bear," but the lesson learned or phenomenon explained will mirror the original version.

Essay Set 8: Travels in Space and Time (presented on page 197)

Students are fascinated with time travel. There are numerous movies and television shows which are based upon this concept, and I find students immediately become excited about the prospect of entering a time machine. These two essays are based upon the theme of astronomy and space travel.

The first essay is explained in the chapter, Sample Assignments. It does not have any direct link to the content area but is related to science units on energy, physics, and astronomy.

The second essay is reflective in that students will imagine themselves to be eighty years into the future, thus being ninety-two years old old. They will be telling their life stories to their grandchildren. To do this effectively, they must imagine the technological advances which will conceivably take place during their lifetimes.

The Year-long Plan: Step 4

Once writing assignments have been determined, it is a matter of pulling vocabulary from various content and literature units to complete each writing unit. Imagine beginning a school year with eight sets of writing assignments organized and ready to distribute, lists of vocabulary words related to each assignment, and an organized calendar of when you will begin and end each content unit. Also imagine organizing your time to eliminate correcting assignments during your busy times of the year.

I have used this approach for many years, and I can attest to thoroughness and stress-relieving benefits of this method. Adopting the philosophy of this book in teaching students to write effectively will not only make you a more complete teacher, but it will also bring to you a new level of organization and a feeling of control over your professional life.

Opening and Closing Paragraphs

The most important component in any essay, composition, or story is the opening paragraph. It is at this point that the reader asks, "Do I keep reading or do I stop?" Given this, students need a lot of practice writing opening paragraphs using the various methods for creating interest (also referred to as a "hook").

The opening paragraph must also include the "thesis." If there is any uncertainty as to what a thesis is, it will become very clear in this chapter. My preference is to have students state the thesis within one sentence, although opinions do vary. Some teachers want students to write one sentence for each thesis item. To me, this seems to give the reader too much information about the item, thus lessening the need to read the remainder of the essay. Regardless of which approach you take, the thesis is an essential component in the opening paragraph.

The next most important ingredient in any writing assignment is the closing paragraph. A good essay or story is like a sandwich with the opening and closing paragraphs providing the "bread" that holds the writing together. I like to have my students practice writing openings and closings as a unit. They are closely linked — similar, yet different. The closing paragraph ideally has three components. The "link" typically begins the closing and is a connection or continuation of the opening hook (interest). The student must then "restate" the thesis in different words, and should end the paper with a "twist." The twist is a final sentence which causes the reader to nod in approval or smile in agreement.

I teach my students that there are six ways in which to create interest in an opening paragraph: a personal anecdote, three questions, a quote (song lyric, poem, etc.), unusual fact(s), a biographical recollection, and in the middle of a story. Within each of these approaches, there are ways to distribute or share the interest between the opening and closing paragraphs.

The Personal Anecdote

In almost any essay, report, or composition, a personal story or anecdote is a very desirable way to begin. It allows the writer to personalize the writing and show a connection to the topic at hand.

For example, if a fourth grader were writing about George Washington, he might discuss a personal visit to the Washington Monument or Mount Vernon, describe a time when he suffered due to freezing weather (as at Valley

Forge), imagine himself to be a child on the street with Washington and his men riding by on their way to battle, or reveal a time when he believed in and supported a cause due to a personal conviction.

A seventh grader writing a science project comparing the chemical composition of coal and diamonds might begin with a story describing a time he or she was watching a television commercial about a diamond substitute in a ring (a diamondoid), an occasion when he or she was entrusted with something of value and misplaced it, or a situation in which two items which were similar in name or consistency created a problem (for example, using baking soda instead of baking powder in a recipe or using aerosol oven cleaner instead of furniture polish to "wax" the dining room table). The goal is to allow the writer to put himself or herself into the writing and allow the reader to be a part of the experience.

One interesting aspect of these anecdotes is that they need not be true. Some teachers may take offense to this approach, but when one thinks about it, eight to fifteen year old children have not had that many life experiences. Sometimes, we must give them leeway to be creative in the pursuit of interesting writing.

When students begin an essay with a personal anecdote, there are a number of ways in which they can link to the closing paragraph. One option is to tell a portion of the story in the first three or four sentences of the opening paragraph and complete the story in the closing paragraph. The caveat is that after several body paragraphs, the student cannot simply jump to the story again in the closing. There has to be a transition statement to blend the body paragraphs to the anecdote.

A second approach is to finish the story in the opening paragraph (three or four sentences) and in the closing, share the effects or consequences of the incident. This might be the lesson learned, the knowledge gained, or the impact upon others.

A third method is to explain what the student did to assure that the mistake, lesson, or experience did not reoccur the next time the same situation presented itself.

Regardless of the approach chosen by the student, after the "link" to the anecdote in the closing paragraph has been made, the student must restate the thesis in different words.

In terms of the placement of the anecdote in the closing, an approach that a more accomplished writer may take is to begin the final paragraph with a restate of the thesis. The author could then use one of the linking techniques described above to complete, interpret, or analyze the personal anecdote. The final ingredient is to add a thought provoking or humorous touch to end the paper (twist).

Examples

Topic: A report on George Washington
Opening Paragraph: A personal anecdote

It seemed that all we did was drive, and each time we stopped, it was to visit another historical site. That morning in Washington

D.C. was different. We stepped out of our hotel and walked four or five blocks. Suddenly, I was amazed by all that surrounded me, the Capitol building off the distance, the White House to my left, a vast field of grass and two ponds reflecting a towering white monument. "What's that?" I asked my dad, and he responded, "That's the Washington monument, in memory of George Washington." My mind started to wander, "A monument, a city named in his honor, this must be someone who made a difference," As I began to learn more about his courage, his leadership, and his patriotism, I realized he had indeed accomplished much.

Closing Paragraph: Completes the story of the personal anecdote

"Washington," when I hear the word, I'm never quite certain what I think of first: the man, the city, or the monument. That day when I first saw the monument, my family and I climbed hundreds of steps to try to reach the lookout tower. Unfortunately, my little sister got tired, my mom got a blister, and we all had to walk down without reaching our destination. We returned to the hotel and the next morning loaded the car and started driving. I wish we had made it to the top, and I wish we had a few more days to spend in Washington D.C. I realized that the historical sights I saw that summer were more than buildings. They represented people with vision, a commitment to a new country, and a willingness to sacrifice everything for something I took for granted — my freedom.

Closing Paragraph: Effect, consequence, lesson learned, or knowledge gained

We take so much for granted as Americans. I can sit in a car and go anywhere, eat any food I choose, dress the way I want, and yet, I complain that I have to visit another historical site. I realize more every day that George Washington would never have accepted such an attitude. His sense of perseverance, his love of country, and his ability to convince those around him to rise to the occasion would not let him take anything for granted. We all learn from our experiences, and that day at the Washington monument made me realize that perhaps learning a little bit about American history wasn't so bad after all.

Closing Paragraph: Avoid making the same mistake again

Three days later we left Washington D.C. with my parents in the best moods they had been in for months. I know it all had to do with my change of attitude and the fact they felt I suddenly appreciated their efforts rather than groaning with every application of the brake pedal. I don't know what exactly happened, but there was something about the Washington monument and the city of Washington D.C. that changed me. I won't swear that I'll never complain again, but thanks to the conviction, commitment, and concern of Americans like George Washington, I do know that I'll think twice before I take all that I have for granted.

Three Questions

This is probably my least favorite method of creating interest, but for many students it is a safe and foolproof approach. Many teachers teach students to begin with a single question. I don't believe one question gives the reader enough to think about and also limits the writer to a very brief opening.

Some students begin their essays with one question. To lengthen the paragraph, they often answer the question within the opening and in so doing, give away the purpose of the entire essay or composition. A much more effective approach is to ask three questions in the opening and then provide brief answers in the closing paragraph.

There are two ways to present the three questions: begin with a specific question and become more general with each of the next two, or begin with a general question and then focus the next two questions on more specific ideas.

The benefit of moving from specific to general is that typically the reader is caught off-guard (thus gaining interest) by the intensity or unusual wording of the first question. The desire is to read more and find out where the writer is headed. The general concept to the specific method accomplishes the same goal, but with each question, the reader becomes more focused on the intent of the paper.

In both cases, teach students that each question must begin with a different word or phrase. It is very ineffective and cumbersome to read three consecutive questions which all begin similarly.

There are only two ways which I have discovered to link questions in the closing paragraph. Typically, the most effective is to answer the questions or to restate the questions in the form of an answer. A second approach is to reword the questions or to consolidate the three questions into one and then provide a brief response. It is especially effective if the response to the consolidated question is a restate of the thesis. This has a way of bringing all aspects of the paper together in a very neat package in the final paragraph.

To provide a twist in an essay that begins with questions, one can either refer to the process of asking and answering questions, or one can ask a final question which the paper has answered. One caveat: Be certain students do not close with a question or statement which focuses the reader on a new problem or new information. Students do this often, and it completely undermines their entire paper. The message sent to the reader is, "You wasted your time reading this because the real problem is ...."

Examples

Topic: Agribusiness is devouring the small farmer
Opening Paragraph: General question to specific question

Is it true that bigger is always better? Could it be that our insatiable desire for more is in many ways giving us less? Once we have accepted the premise that more choice is better, is it possible to ever reverse that trend or have we set a course from which there is no turning back? For the family-owned variety store downtown, the independent mechanic around the corner, and for the mom 'n' pop eatery on the outskirts of town, more and bigger has been anything but better. Perhaps no one has been so affected by this "more, more, more" philosophy tham the American farmer. The need to do more with less, to compete with agribusiness, and maintain a market share has become almost impossible. The American tradition of the family farm is part of Americana which is dying before our eyes.

Closing Paragraph: Answer the questions

Many of us, while driving past the new Super Wal-marts or Super K-Marts, would respond that bigger is not necessarily better.

When I walk inside one of these behemoths and find they do not have what I want or are out of stock, I have no other place to look since they have driven the other stores in my area out of business. I am also afraid that this is a trend which will never be reversed. I doubt if the corner five and dime will ever reopen in our town. I also doubt the farming families that used to scratch out a living in rural America will ever again struggle to keep the tractor running, keep tabs on the changing prices of wheat or corn, or work together as a family during harvest time to bring in the crop. Wall street profit has replaced the country road existence. Unfortunately, for our country, the roads will be forever closed.

Topic: UFO's, fact or fiction?

Opening Paragraph: Specific question to general question

Did you see that eerie green light flashing in the sky last night? Have you ever scanned the night's sky and seen something that couldn't be explained? Has anyone ever actually seen a UFO, or is it just our imaginations running wild with tricks played by mother nature? For the past forty years rumors have run rampant regarding the existence of unidentified flying objects. The number of people who have reported similar phenomenon, the secrecy of the American government, and the simple fact that it seems highly improbable that Earth is the only inhabited planet convinces me that UFO's are indeed real.

Closing Paragraph: Consolidating questions into one and providing an answer.

The evening news or morning paper might minimize the green lights as an atmospheric condition caused by heat lighting seen through the smoke of a far away forest fire. The reports of sightings of unidentified flying objects will forever be squelched by the mainstream media as emissaries of governmental agencies. For the citizens who peered up in the sky and saw unexplainable streaks and flashes and heard bizarre sounds, UFOs will continue to be reported and discussed. To at least half of all Americans, there is something out there, something the government is keeping secret. Maybe it can't yet be proven, but many great discoveries have been a result of not letting the skeptics undermine one's beliefs.

Quotation, Song Lyric, or Poem

Beginning an essay or composition with a quote is a tried and true method. If the student can find an appropriate connection to the topic at hand, it is a very effective unifying element.

However, I often find my students discover or create an interesting quotation and then do not quite know what to do with it. Using a quote effectively probably takes more practice than any other method of creating interest. I require my students begin several essays each year with a quote, others with a poem or thought, and others with a song lyric. This provides the continual practice they need.

One of the first approaches I teach students is that there is nothing sacred or magical about a quotation. Some of the best quotes I have read to begin papers have been created by the student. They often ask, "Should I say, 'That is a quote I made up last week?'" I explain that a better approach might be, "I remember hearing this quote somewhere."

When one analyzes this, isn't it more realistic to have a student write, "I remember hearing this when I was young," as opposed to, "This is a famous quote by the great Spanish author, Cervantes." This is not to infer that students should not use the quotes of others, but if they can find nothing appropriate, I tell them to make it up!

Once a quote is written, students can expand upon the meaning by interpreting it in their own words, restating the quote in different words, telling a brief personal story of how the quote affected their lives, giving an example to support their interpretation, imagining what the author was trying to accomplish, picking out specific words to analyze more thoroughly, or explaining why they disagree with the quote. Regardless of the approach, the next step in the opening paragraph is to connect the quote to the topic of the essay.

In writing the closing paragraph, students can make a choice of which approach will most effectively link the opening and closing paragraphs. For example, if a student provided an interpretation in the opening, he or she might restate the quote in different words to begin the closing. If specific words were analyzed in the opening, the writer might suggest or insert different words in the closing and then briefly discuss the impact of these subtle changes.

Obviously, there are a number of ways to combine these approaches. Once again, students need to practice writing various combinations in class.

Examples

Topic: The creativity of Dr. Seuss
Opening Paragraph: Interpreting in your own words

"Words paint in the colors that have never been seen." I heard this quote while flipping through the channels on the television one night. As I began to ponder its meaning, other thoughts began to surface: "Are there sounds that have never been heard or emotions that have never been experienced?" I'm not certain if any of this is realistic, but they are wonderful concepts for the imagination to work on. Many writers aspire to provide unimagined or unseen colors for their readers but none so uniquely as Theodor Geisel, better known as Dr. Seuss. His ability to imagine the unseen, rhyme the unrhymable, and draw the non-existent set him apart from the mainstream of children's writers.

Opening Paragraph: Restate in different words

"Words paint in the colors that have never been seen." What a sad world it would be if this were not the case. Think of the limits we would place upon ourselves if we limited words to tell us only what is real. I believe there are countless ideas that have never been imagined and dreams that have never been realized. Maybe, in part, this belief or hope comes from my reading books by Dr. Seuss. He created images which took me to places I'd never been, let me picture characters who could never be imagined, and mesmerized me with sounds that I still can hear today.

Opening Paragraph: Brief personal story

"Words paint in colors that have never been seen." According to my fifth grade teacher, Mrs. Bell, my words painted in colors no one would ever want to see. I'll never forget that first "creative" story I wrote for her and my response when she put me down in front of the whole class. "What did you expect, writing like Madeleine L'Engle?" "No," she retorted, "just something better than Dr. Seuss!" Suddenly, all of my classmates rallied to my support. Her Dr. Seuss comment had struck a nerve and rightfully so. If any author ever wrote words that expressed unseen colors, it was Dr. Seuss.

46

Opening Paragraph: Example to support

"Words paint in colors that have never been seen." This quotation is undoubtedly true. For example, when one considers a description such as, "As I peered below, the lights of the city were so bright that they created unimaginable shadows in the night sky," images of intermingling blacks and greys flood the imagination. Yet, there seems to be more. Somehow, there is light that, at least in my mind, transforms colors I can imagine into something new and different. Such is the power of words. As a child, I remember one author who could always create a new array of colors — Dr. Seuss. His playful art, unusual imagination, and mastery of rhythm always took me to places never before imagined.

Opening Paragraph: Intent of the author

"Words paint in colors that have never been seen." This quote is like candy for the imagination. I feel certain the author was trying to play a word game to entice or cajole the reader into wrestling for a deeper meaning. To me, the meaning is obvious, that is, words go beyond the senses. While some authors might struggle to describe what colors have never been seen, Dr. Seuss took the essence of this quote to heart. He played with words, toyed with images and constructed unimaginable places.

Opening Paragraph: Analyzing specific words

"Words paint in colors that have never been seen." A definite conflict of purpose immediately surfaces as one reads this quote. Artists paint, and they can only paint in those colors that the human eye perceives. To many, this quote would not make any sense at all. However, to Theodor Geisel, better known as Dr. Seuss, this thought was a way of life. His words created colors, his rhymes fostered sensations, and his rhythms generated sounds never seen, felt, or heard before.

Opening Paragraph: Why you disagree (or agree).

"Words paint in the colors that have never been seen." When one analyzes what this quote is actually saying, it parallels the absurd question often asked at parties, "If a tree falls in the forest, does it make a noise?" Now it is certain that words can create moods, stimulate emotions, and undoubtedly help us to envision colors, but only the colors known to our experience. Many authors do this well; in fact, children's authors are often the best at stimulating one's imagination. Raold Dahl, Maurice Sendak, and Shel Silverstein are certainly masters but probably no one has been more successful than Dr. Seuss. His words, his rhyme, and his art never created unseen colors, but they certainly made red richer, yellow brighter, and black deeper than what we typically see.

Unusual or Bizarre Fact

This approach is similar to beginning with three questions except that in this case, the writer introduces some unusual, mind-catching fact or statistic that throws the reader off-guard. It can be stretched to two or three facts as long as each fact is on the same topic and each becomes more specific. I have had students try to introduce three different unusual facts at the outset, but it never seems to work particularly well.

48

Facts generally capture our imaginations and curiosity. Calendars are sold which present an unusual fact for the day. Computer enthusiasts surf internet sites which present daily "factoids." The supermarket check-out line is stocked with tabloids which present mind-numbing "facts" to attract the shoppers' attention. Obviously, using this a technique to begin an essay makes sense.

Once the student has found an interesting or unusual fact, the next step, of course, is to blend the fact into the essay topic. I find that since the fact is closely related to the subject of the essay, students do this fairly readily.

To add a link or concluding statement in the closing paragraph, the student might provide another, related fact, could give an example to explain the fact in a different way, give an example as to why the fact might be misinterpreted or unreliable, or reword the fact for a different perspective in hopes of showing how the fact supports the thesis or purpose of the paper.

Examples

Topic: A study of insects
Opening Paragraph: A bizarre fact

It is generally accepted that humans are the most intelligent animals on earth; however, when one considers that for every human, there are over one million ants, or that the world's termite population outweighs the human population ten to one, we begin to get the perspective that we may be smart, but we'd better be careful! Most people have probably said, "I hate bugs," at some point, but without those little six-legged critters, the world would be a very different place.

Closing Paragraph: Rewording the fact from a different perspective

Insects may outnumber and outweigh humans by vast margins, but we maintain our advantage over them by using just three pounds of our body mass — our brains. When one of these small intruders gets too close to us, we prevail due to our intellect or our strength. As long as we are confident that we can keep insects in check, we may as well learn to accept that without them, nature's cycle of decay, survival of the fittest, and natural selection would be placed so drastically out of balance that we would cease to exist.

Topic: Choosing a lifelong career
Opening Paragraph: An unusual statistic

Bill Gates, founder of Microsoft, could spend one million dollars per day, every day, seven days per week, and would not run out of money until he was 311 years old! Most would agree that he has reached a point of financial security. In fact, it would be almost impossible to figure out how one could spend one million dollars per day. This spending dilemma is not a problem that will be faced by most of us as we enter the world of work. For most Americans, finding an occupation that is satisfying, earning enough money to live comfortably, and figuring out a realistic blend between work and leisure are three essential factors in beginning one's career.

Closing Paragraph: How the fact might be misinterpreted

It is doubtful that when Bill Gates started designing and producing software that his goal was to become the richest man in the world. It is also doubtful that Bill Gates could physically put his hands on one million dollars day after day. His wealth is a composite of stock value, unpaid dividends, and real property that would need to be sold before dollar bills came into play. Bill Gates and the average contented worker are successful in their careers not because of the money, but because when they get up in the morning, their work is interesting, rewarding, and blends, rather than overshadows, their personal lives. If we learn to work at jobs in which we give more than we take, there will be no need to worry about the money we make.

Biographical Recollection

This is very similar to a personal anecdote yet provides much leeway because a student may write about anyone — a relative, friend, historical figure, celebrity, or a fictitious character. The subject matter is limitless.

The point of view can be first person (I) or omniscient (he/she/they). This is the first decision students must make when they begin writing using this approach: "Do I know the person, or do I know *about* the person?"

Once again, it is important that students realize this is not a report or essay about that person; it is merely a means of creating interest to absorb the reader in the topic at hand. I will provide some examples of how students might approach this.

If a fourth grader were writing a paper on a difficult decision that he or she has made, a biographical introduction might begin with a story of an historical leader who made a very difficult decision. He or she might imagine the President of the United States deciding whether or not to send troops into war, or an explorer deciding which direction to take in a given situation.

If a sixth grader were writing an essay trying to convince the reader that the school year should be increased from 180 days to 200 days, he or she might provide a biographical sketch of a successful Japanese business person who attributed his or her success to the rigors of the longer Japanese school year and school day. Another approach would be to write about Davy Crockett, who purportedly never went to school. The student might contrast how life has changed, and how Davy Crockett would not have a chance for success in today's society.

Writing the closing paragraph in a biographical introduction again is similar to the personal anecdote. The writer now has a chance to "sandwich" the essay with a second mention of the character, to give another story, or embellish the original anecdote. Quite often, the biographical character provides an excellent means for a twist or clever closing to the essay.

Make certain that students differentiate between the personal anecdote and biographical incident. They are different approaches, and both can be used very effectively in almost any formal writing.

Examples
Topic: The value of fairy tales in children's lives
Opening Paragraph: A grandparent as an inspiration

Every summer, I looked forward to spending four or five weeks at my grandparents' farm in Nebraska. It wasn't that I wanted to be away from my friends, but I did love being around my grandparents, especially my "Grampa Ed" as I called him. Each night he would put me to bed and tell me a story about magical worlds, people, and events. He had a way, with his deep voice, of making me believe that all of this magic was really possible. I learned a lot over those years from the stories that he told. They taught me that there is always hope, that kindness is rewarded, and that in times of darkness, a dream world can be very comforting.

Closing Paragraph: Completing the story

The last story I remember my Grampa Ed telling me was about a king who loved his son very much but had to go away for a very long time. It was a sad story, but the way Grampa told it taught me a lesson that even though people who love one another are apart, in a way they are always together. It made sense when he said it and makes even more sense now. That was my last trip to Nebraska and was the last time I saw Grampa Ed. But he was right, he is always with me giving me a purpose, a way to live, and a place to go when I need a refuge. Fairy tales may not come true, but they do teach us about truth.

In the Middle of a Story

Again, this is similar to a personal anecdote, but in this case, the story or event is already in progress. It is almost as if the reader were late in joining a group that has been listening to the writer's description. Often, this approach will begin with a transitional words such as while or since. It might also begin with a verbal: "Tired, I quickly..." or "Swimming seemed like...". These beginnings provide a sense of instant involvement for the reader.

Students must be cautioned that the propose of beginning with the incident is solely to hook the reader. This must be done in two or three sentences, and the writer must then use a sentence to transition to the thesis. Being concise while telling a story is a challenge for most students. They need practice in choosing what to leave in and what to exclude.

In the closing paragraph, the writer has several options. He or she may complete the story or action, return to the beginning of the story and give the background of how he or she arrived in the predicament, tell the reader what was learned from the experience, or explain how a different reaction might have generated an alternative result.

Examples

Topic: Autobiography
Opening Paragraph: In the middle of a hiking trip

It couldn't have been any hotter that afternoon as I neared the mountain's peak. I was two or three hundred yards ahead of my two hiking partners, and the only thing that kept me going was the knowledge that if I kept putting one foot in front of the other, I would be the first to reach the summit. Sweat dripped from every pore in my body, and my throat burned with thirst. Why was I doing this, I wondered. It seems that throughout my life I have continually put myself in situations in which I was proving myself. Whether it was my first recollection as a small child, an ill-fated attempt to break a world's record, or my first summer at camp, it was always me against the world.

Closing Paragraph: Completing the story

In my mind there is nothing greater than a personal challange. That sweltering hike to the mountain top ended just as I would have wanted it to. I reached the top and had time to regain my composure as I watched my two weary comrades make their final ascent to meet me. The three of us stood together, proud of our accomplishment. There was an extra sense of achievement because I had been first. Where this competitive attitude comes from I am uncertain, but I do know that it started when I was young. From my first memory to my summertime leisure activities, there has always been a burning desire to win. I know that winning isn't everything, but for me, it has a certain something unmatched by any other feeling.

There are undoubtedly other interesting ways to create interest for the reader. The ideas presented here are the six that I teach my students.

One aspect to keep in mind when teaching opening and closing paragraphs is that there are occasions when a student writes an essay and must get right to the point. When I meet with high school teachers who teach advanced placement classes, they remind me that the formula for AP test responses is to begin the first sentence by stating the problem and then move right into the thesis. I am certain they are correct.

The point that I continually emphasize is that for third through ninth graders, the formula is very different than for the high school senior.

We must emphasize the concept of the sandwich; that is, the opening and closing paragraph holding the essay together with a common theme. If we teach the opening paragraph with two ingredients: create interest and provide a clear thesis; and the closing paragraph with three components: link to the interest, restate the thesis in different words, and add a twist, students have a model for almost every type of writing they will ever do.

When the structure and organization of writing is no longer mystical, the writing students can do can be magical.

Body Paragraphs

If the opening and closing paragraphs are the bread which create the top and bottom of the sandwich, the body paragraphs are the substance that makes the sandwich worth consuming. Interestingly, I believe that if the opening and closing are very well written, the body can be less effective and still please the reader. The body is the third most important component of an essay.

If the writer has done an effective job of clearly stating a thesis in the opening paragraph, the reader is already focused and interested in what he or she is about to read. The body paragraphs must accomplish three major tasks. They must explain and give examples to prove the thesis, they must flow smoothly from one paragraph to the next through use of transitions, and each paragraph must describe a specific aspect of the story. In this chapter, we will take a more specific look at each of these ingredients.

Many times, my students come to me with two or three sentences of a body paragraph and explain that there is nothing else to say. My response is always the same: examples, examples, and more examples. Writing and saying something is true does not make it true. We begin to believe when examples are given which prove the point. If students are writing a descriptive essay and want to discuss the look of snow on a cold winter's morning, what more can they say than it was white and cold? There are a myriad of examples they can give. What was the visual texture of the snow? What were the colors of the shadows? How did the snow cover the physical terrain? What shapes were created? What sound was heard as they walked? What does cold smell like? etc. Convincing the reader does not come from saying it is cold, it comes from letting the reader imagine the scene through vivid wordings or observations. Examples are the only way to prove the point you are making.

The second essential aspect of body paragraphs is that they must read smoothly from one paragraph to the next. In the standard five paragraph essay, I require students to check for the following:

1. Use a transition statement in either the second or third body paragraph — not both. Transitions begin with words like since, while, in addition to, as, etc. (there is a complete list of common transition words on page 76).
2. Never end a paragraph with an introduction of the next paragraph's topic. Transitions or the topic sentence belong in the first sentence of the paragraph.

3. Avoid using a closing sentence in every body paragraph. You need not recap all you have said within the final sentence. If, however, a body paragraph seems to end too abruptly, then consider a clincher sentence based upon the topic of that paragraph.

4. Never use phrases like, "In the next paragraph," "In this essay," "I just told you why...," or, "Now I'm going to..." Do not talk to the reader, and do not talk about your essay.

5. Be certain that every body paragraph begins with a different word or phrase.

6. Check the sentence length in each body paragraph. Use a combination of simple, compound, and complex sentences.

When I speak to groups of teachers and share lists as presented above, I sometimes get the question, "What about creativity? Aren't you limiting the students' ability by holding them to such a structured concept?"

As expressed before, I believe that creativity is enhanced within a structure. When students have a consistent outline or "formula," they can do remarkable writing as they stretch the boundaries. We must provide specific guidelines because in so doing, we create a safety net. Many students are afraid to try if they have no boundaries. The more clear and structured our directions, the better the students' writing will be.

One of the most glaring faults I find when students write the body paragraphs of their essays is they often have paragraphs which overlap in content; they say the same thing twice. The fundamental problem here is not the body paragraphs, it is that the thesis has not delineated specifically enough.

Students usually do not realize this until they start writing the body paragraphs, and all of a sudden, they conclude that there is not enough different information to merit a separate paragraph. Let us look at some examples.

Topic: An adventure in a time machine (note that topics can be very creative and still warrant a thesis)

Thesis: As my experimental machine ground to a halt, I could not help but wonder what the environment, the fashion, and the living conditions would be in this future society.

This thesis clearly focuses the body paragraphs on three distinct topics; however, the writer may drift in the environment paragraph and make mention of how this affected living conditions. That is the type of overlap which must be avoided. The thesis statement will work, but the writer must take care to keep each paragraph unique.

Thesis: As my experimental machine ground to a halt, thoughts raced through my mind as to how life, the people, and the houses had changed.

This is very typical of the type of thesis statement students write before they realize that each thesis item must be very distinct. In this case, I would ask the writer how he or she will differentiate between the life and people. I would encourage the student to combine these two topics into one, widen the "houses" topic into perhaps the "architecture," and add a third, completely different topic to the thesis.

Thesis: As my experimental machine ground to a halt, I began to wonder how the world had changed.

My concern with this thesis is that there is no itemized focus for the paper and very little direction or anticipation for the reader. The topic is so broad that the student will most likely ramble on and on about different topics, repeating information from one paragraph to the next.

Referring again to my experience in using this approach, fellow teachers will question the structure of the thesis. "You mean everything students write should have a clearly stated thesis in which topics are listed?" Other than in a story, my response is, yes. A clear thesis gives students a purpose and direction. It also forces them into that fundamental decision of categorizing and itemizing a topic. This is essential for young writers.

There will come a time in a student's writing career when the thesis can become less specific — in the upper high school years. At this point, the student has had practice writing many essays, reports, and compositions; has learned to categorize and itemize topics; has mastered the challenge of keeping each body paragraph to a specific topic; knows how to create interest and summarize a thesis in the opening and closing paragraphs; and has mastered the mechanics of writing.

Until a student has reached this level of proficiency (I believe only about one in five graduating high school seniors attain this plateau), every extended writing assignment should be as structured as those I describe in this book.

Sample Body Paragraphs

My first few steps from my machine made me shudder as I absorbed the environment that surrounded me. Everywhere I looked there was concrete — no flowers, no grass, no planters with trees, just grey concrete. It was stark, flat, and completely lacking in texture, very unlike the stained and cracked sidewalks from my time. In the distance there were rolling hills, but they seemed to have no life. It was an endless expanse of brown dirt without bushes, trees, or any dimension. It was as if I were looking at sand dunes but without any of the windswept ravines or angular ridges that made them interesting or beautiful. The sky was a dull greyish blue with a few clouds that erased any reflection of color or for that matter, hope. It was a world so devoid of inspiration that I wondered why it existed.

There were people who occasionally passed me but paid absolutely no attention to my stares or my obvious look of dismay. I was in jeans, tennis shoes, and T-shirt with a bright red shirt unbuttoned and untucked. All who passed were dressed in a jumpsuit-like costume in random colors of beige, pale yellow, mint green, and grey. It was as if I had walked into a factory of uniformed workers whose bosses thought it more productive to have employees dressed as simply and as drably as possible. My clothing stuck out like neon, but no one looked at me or even reflected a hint of interest or surprise. They wore their hair at a similar length as mine, but there seemed to be no differentiation between hair length in males or females, and the outfits they wore gave no indication that women, men or children were interested in any type of style, fashion, or trend.

While the environment and fashion lacked any intrigue or interest, I knew there had to be more to this world which I had invaded. I entered a doorway, and it was as if I had discovered a different world. Brilliant colored lights illuminated every corner of the huge expanse. The dull colors of the jumpsuits came alive with fluorescence and shimmering taffeta designs as the wearers moved about the room. People smiled and chatted in friendly tones that I understood. There were words that were new, but I could understand the gist of the conversations I overheard. Still, no one paid any attention to me, but children would race by with giggles and screams, and the adults seemed to have no fear that I would do any harm to anyone. It was as if their personalities only came alive when they were inside. The external world was simply a means of getting from one place to another. Once they entered an enclosed environment, life began again. I knew there was much more to learn about this place, but at least my original despair had been replaced with a sense that maybe there was hope for the future after all.

To these paragraphs, the student would add an opening and closing as described in the previous chapter. In reading these body paragraphs, the transition in the third paragraph is obvious, the use of examples are numerous, sentence structure is varied, and paragraphs are clearly focused upon specific topics which inter-relate but never repeat. There is a definite formula, yet the writer is very creative and descriptive.

Students can use this format whether they are writing a book report, a report of information, a science project, an autobiographical essay, a narrative, or a interpretive composition. The point I am trying to make is that regardless of the domain, the structure of the essay remains the same. All students can learn to write using this approach.

To briefly summarize this section on body paragraphs, the key features are: When in doubt, give examples; avoid repetition; and transition smoothly.

Punctuation

Commas, periods, question marks, hyphens, aprostrophes — those little marks we have come to know and love! Each year we diligently teach them, and each year our students stare blankly at us wondering where those magical punctuation marks are supposed to go. I have taught punctuation for many years, but only in the last two years have I done an effective job. I finally realized that there were just too many rules and too many exceptions.

I began to combine and simplify the rules to as few and as universal as possible. I now have students memorize this numbered system of rules. When I correct a paper, if a student has a missing or unnecessary comma or semicolon, all I need to do is write in the punctuation mark with the rule number above the error. This is a true time saver in correcting papers. My students know the rules from memory, but I also·list the rules on a wall chart in the classroom, and students have the rules written in their notebooks.

As with any standardization or simplification, one can always add, "But what about...." For my students, these rules work very well.

The Ten Comma Rules

1. Use a comma to offset introductory words, phrases, or clauses.

This rule is easy to remember because an introduction always comes first, hence rule one. If I were teaching third or fourth graders, I would simplify this rule to, "Use a comma to offset introductory words." In the fifth grade, I would add, "Use a comma to offset an introductory word or phrase." Sixth graders should learn the complete rule.

Examples
Yesterday, I walked home from school.
In the corner, a young man stood.
When I first saw her, I knew I would marry her.

One should always use a comma after an introductory word or clause. Some words which must be offset are: yes, no, today, surely, indeed, well, however, and meanwhile. There are many others as well.

Most older students readily understand the use of exclamation marks, but one unique usage can be taught while presenting comma rule one. An exclamation mark may be used instead of a comma after an introductory word if the word is shouted or emphasized. Note below that the word after the exclamation is capitalized; the word after a comma is not.

Examples

Hurry! The train is leaving soon!

Oh! You never thought of that!

Hurry, the train is leaving soon!

Oh, you never thought of that!

Introductory clauses which must be offset with a comma are actually subordinate clauses (also called dependent clauses). They begin with subordinate conjunctions. To be more specific, they are also usually adverbial clauses. Some samples of subordinate conjunctions include: after, although, as, because, before, even if, even though, except, if, in order that, since, though, unless, until, when, whenever, wherever, whether, and while.

There are four basic types of phrases: prepositional, gerund, participial, and infinitive. Nine times out of ten, the introductory phrase is prepositional. The next most common use is the infinitive phrase (a verb with "to" attached — to run, to be, etc.). The participial (a verb with an "ing" or "ed" ending which functions as an adjective) can be used as an introductory phrase but almost always with the "ing" (present) form and rarely with the "ed" (past form). The gerund (a verb with an "ing" ending which functions as a noun, i.e. walking is fun) is almost impossible to use as an introductory phrase. Each of these is typically offset by a comma when used to begin a sentence

Examples

Prepositional:	On the surface, he appeared calm.
Participial:	Seeing the result, he decided to quit.
Infinitive:	To be successful, one must study.

2. Use a comma between two descriptive adjectives which can be reversed in order (or can have "and" placed between them.)

This rule is quite obvious, and after memorization and a few examples, I find students have very little trouble with comma rule two. It helps if students have a knowledge of the different types of adjectives.

Examples

The old, red wagon was broken. ("red, old" or "old and red")

The five silver spoons were on the table. ("Silver, five" or "five and silver" do not work. Also, five is a limiting adjective.)

You can help students memorize this rule by reminding them that rule two requires two adjectives.

3. Use a comma between three or more items in a series.

This is one of the first comma rules that young students learn. It is straight-forward, and there should be no exceptions. Unfortunately, the punctuation gurus who alter existing writing rules have declared that the last comma (before "and") is now optional. We have thus added confusion to a rule which was black and white. I prefer to have students always include the comma before the conjunction.

4. Use a comma before "and, but, or, nor, for, yet" if there is a complete sentence (independent clause) on either side.

This is one rule that students repeatedly miss. One of my final checks on an essay before it is handed in is to have students search out every coordinating conjunction (and, but, or, nor, for, yet) and decide whether or not a comma is necessary. When the students apply this rule, they are identifying a compound sentence. This is the type of specific direction we must give our students. They must be looking for something tangible as they proofread.

One pitfall to this rule is that the second independent clause must have subject. If there is no subject (if it begins with a verb) a comma is unnecessary.

A second important reminder is that only the six coordinating conjunctions require a comma. Quite often, students tell me that former teachers have instructed them to use a comma before words like: so, because, if, since, etc. These are subordinating conjunctions and begin a subordinate or dependent clause, thus creating a complex sentence. Subordinating conjunctions do not require a comma when they connect two clauses.

Examples

He bought his mother a present, and he brought his sister a rose. (Comma is necessary.)

He bought his mother a present and brought his sister a rose. (Comma is not necessary.)

He bought his mother a present because he brought his sister a rose. (Comma is not necessary.)

It is unnecessary to add the comma if the two independent clauses are very short.

Example

He talked and I listened.

5. Use a comma to offset unnecessary and parenthetical words, phrases, and clauses; appositives; and words in direct address.

I will confess, this is an all-inclusive rule, but the words used in each of these classifications are unnecessary to the overall structure of the sentence. It makes it much easier for students to simply decide if a word, phrase, or clause is unnecessary in the sentence, and if so, they need to add

70

commas. This sometimes generates a discussion of the "restrictive versus non-restrictive clause." I am not convinced that elementary students need worry about these terms.

Examples

We were, in short, surprised by the results. (unnecessary or parenthetical)

Mr. Williams, our math teacher, is not at school today. (appositive)

We regret, Ms. Johnston, that your order was not sent on time. (direct address)

There is one minor exception. Very closely related appositives do not need a comma, "My cousin Mary," or "Louis the Fourth."

6. Use a comma between days, dates, and years.

Examples

Monday, February 4, 2003

January 8, 2001

7. Use a comma in the salutation in a friendly letter.

The distinction needs to be made between a business and a friendly letter. I tell my students that if they call the person by his or her first name, it is a friendly letter, and they must use a comma after the greeting (Dear Jim,). If not, it is a business letter which requires a colon after the greeting (Dear Mr. Smith:). As part of this rule, students must always use a comma after the closing (Yours truly,).

A mnemonic device I use to help students remember rule seven is that l-e-t-t-e-r-s has seven letters. It is silly but I find my students remember it this way.

8. Use a comma between cities and states but not between states and zip codes.

An obvious rule with no explanation necessary. I help them to remember this rule number by pointing out that s-t-a-t-e-z-i-p has eight letters.

9. Use a comma to offset quotations.

Teaching students to write dialogue correctly is very difficult. This rule is covered more thoroughly in the section on quotation marks. I include this with comma rules because often students will forget the comma when using quotes, and I want to be able to remind them by simply writing a "9" above the missing comma on their work. The confusion with this rule is that many times a question or exclamation mark may be substituted for the comma.

10. Use a comma where a natural pause is necessary or to avoid confusing wordings.

This rule is necessary because we often write or say things which require a comma to avoid confusion. Students have a tendency to rely on this rule as a "defense" when they are actually unsure of which rule to use. When I teach rule number ten, I remind students that this application is very rare. If they are writing and feel compelled to use rule ten, it is probably best to reword the entire sentence to make it more clear.

Examples
I asked you to bring dinner, not eat it!

Just the day before, Carlos had purchased the same game.

Where Jim was, was no concern of mine.

For the purists, I will admit that there are comma cases which are not included within these rules. Let me try to justify my omissions.

Use a comma between numbers — hundreds, thousands, etc. Yes, this is a use of the comma, but I believe it is thoroughly covered in math class. I have very few students who have difficulty applying this rule.

Use a comma between names when the last name is given first as in Purdy, Scott. I do not believe in my twenty-seven years of correcting students' writing that I have ever seen the "last name comma first name" usage. I also believe it is common sense to add the comma.

Use a comma to offset a name and a title such as, Roger M. Smith, A.B., Ph.D., senior professor. This is covered in comma rule five, unnecessary information or parenthetical expressions.

Use a comma between two sets of numbers such as, "I bought 20, three inch nails and 20, two inch nails." This is an application of comma rule ten, use a comma to avoid confusion.

Use a comma to offset an inverted phrase in a sentence such as, "For me, there is no correct response." This case is covered in comma rule one, introductory phrases.

It is obvious that any system which takes twenty to twenty-three different comma rules (as I find in typical language books) and simplifies them into ten rules will seem incomplete to some teachers. I firmly believe that by learning to apply these ten rules, students can effectively use commas. To me, simple makes sense.

The Three Semicolon Rules

The semi-colon is sophisticated punctuation and until the fifth or sixth grade, I do not think students need to learn how to use it. Memorization of rules is easy since there is a close correlation to the comma rules.

1. Use a semicolon between two complete sentences (independent clauses) which are not connected by and, but, or, nor, for, yet.

This sounds very much like comma rule four. When I present this to the students, someone usually asks why they cannot simply use a period. This is a logical observation. I try to explain that a semicolon is "softer" than a period, almost like slowing the reader down instead of stopping him. Over the next several essays, semicolons abound! I then have to remind them not to overuse the semicolon.

Example

He bought his mother a present; he brought his sister a rose.

2. Use a semicolon between two complete sentences (independent clauses) connected by words like: however, on the contrary, and meanwhile. Use a comma after the connecting word.

When students begin writing compound sentences, transitional words make their writing sound much more sophisticated. To do this properly, they must use the semicolon.

Examples

I arrived early; however, many had already entered.

Juan was sick; in fact, he had a severe fever.

If you want to see major improvement in the sentence structure of your students' writing, give them the following list of words and tell them that one or two sentences in each paragraph must use a transitional word. Their writing immediately begins to sound more mature.

75

Transitional words

accordingly	afterwards	again
anyhow	besides	consequently
doubtless	eventually	evidently
finally	furthermore	hence
however	indeed	likewise
meanwhile	moreover	namely
nevertheless	next	otherwise
perhaps	possibly	still
therefore	thus	as a result
at last	at the same time	for example
for instance	in any case	in fact
in short	on the contrary	in addition
that is	on the other hand	

3. Use a semicolon between three or more items in a series when the individual items have commas.

This is very similar to comma rule three, making it easy to remember. It also provides a good opportunity to teach the appositive.

Examples

Sam, my brother; Randy, my cousin; and Laura, my sister were at the party last night.

The Uses of the Apostrophe

There are three uses of the apostrophe: to form possessives; to replace a missing letter (as in contractions); and to create plural forms of numbers, letters, symbols, or words

76

out of context. I do not have my students memorize any rules here, but they have to do a lot of practice to master the apostrophe.

1. Use an apostrophe to form a possessive

I know from experience that many teachers have difficulty in teaching this application. The difficult part for students is deciding whether to add the apostrophe before or after the "s." The three rules I teach are:

- If the word is singular, add 's
- If the word is plural and ends in s, add '
- If the word is plural and doesn't end in s, add 's

Examples

The notebook's cover (notebook is singular, so add 's)

The child's toy (child is singular, so add 's)

The notebooks' covers (notebooks is plural and ends in s, so add ')

The children's toys (children is plural, and does not end in s, so add 's)

When I present these rules to students, I often have one or two who ask, "What about names that end in 's'?" The rules of punctuation include the exception, "If a proper noun ends in 's,' the possessive may be formed by adding only the apostrophe (i.e., Bess' and Doris' books)."

The operational word here is "may." It is also correct to say or write "Bess's and Doris's books." I am trying to keep this as simple as possible for students so my rule is to forget about the exception and always add 's for singular possessives.

If you want to say the phrase, "Bess's and Doris's books," does your ear hear "Bess and Doris books or Besses and Dorises books?" My ear definitely tells me Besses and Dorises, but we all hear things differently. The simple approach is that students will always be correct if they add 's to singular forms.

The next trick in teaching the possessive is helping students identify whether the ownership word is singular or plural. When I read a sample sentence to students that says, "Her brother's watch was broken," they often argue that brothers is plural because they hear the "s" in the sentence. When they see the sentence, it is easier to understand.

To solve this, I have students "stretch it out." That is, I'll have them transpose the sentence to, "The watch of her brother was stolen." I then question, "Who owns something?"— brother. "Is it singular or plural?" — singular. Therefore, to form the possessive, add 's: "My brother's watch was stolen."

Examples

"The tree's leaves" becomes "leaves of the tree." (Tree is singular so add 's to tree — the tree's leaves.)

"The babies' cries" becomes "cries of the babies." (Babies is plural and ends is s, so add ' — the babies' cries.)

"The women's purses" becomes "purses of the women." (Women is plural and does not end in s, so add ' — the women's purses.)

When students are in doubt, and I tell them to "stretch it out," they can usually figure out where the apostrophe should be placed. It gives them the way to resolve the dilemma.

2. Use an apostrophe to replace a missing letter.

In most cases, we teach this as a contraction such as doesn't or didn't. Most students learn this quickly and easily. Some unusual contractions which I share with students are: o'clock (of the clock), 'til (until — which can also be written as till), and '99 (1999).

I ask students to use contractions very sparingly in their writing. Contractions have a tendency to make writing look informal. I do not want them to eliminate them completely; I ask that they avoid overuse.

3. Use an apostrophe to form plural forms of numbers, letters, symbols, and words out of context.

This can get a bit confusing for students, and sometimes, I find that they start randomly throwing apostrophes into their writing to form all plurals.

To teach this concept, I write on the board, "How many eights do you have in your telephone number?" I explain that if they write the word "eight," that this rule does not apply; however, if they write the symbol for eight — 8 — and want to make it plural, they must use an apostrophe. "How many 8's do you have in your phone number?" The same applies to, "How many A's do you have in your name and how many ?'s and ;'s did you use in your essay?"

This rule applies when students want to write the plural form of a word which is used out of the context of its meaning. For example: "You have used too many and's and but's in your paragraph," or, "There are a lot of Jim's in the senior class." This is a rule that I have to continually review with many of my students.

Quotation Marks

Some students love to write dialogue. In a story, a few lines of dialogue can help to show personality and can carry the plot for a time, but I instruct students to use dialogue sparingly.

The first item which students must distinguish is the difference between a direct and indirect quote. One of easiest ways to teach this is to tell students that most indirect quotes begin with the word "that." If other words introduce the quote, usually the word "that" can be substituted.

The second rule I teach, before demonstrating the rules for writing quotation marks, is that you must begin a new paragraph every time a different person speaks. When students think quotes, they must think "indent!"

There is one exception. In researching for this book, I discovered that there is no specific rule as to when it is appropriate to write a two-person dialogue within one para-

paragraph. This becomes a matter of "style" required by a school or univerisity.

I teach students that when writing dialogue they must begin a new paragraph for each speaker unless the conversation is only two lines long, and each line is very short. In novels and short stories, I have seen brief dialogue written in a variety of ways. There seems to be no general agreement on the "proper" way.

Other than this exception, the rules for writing quotes are quite consistent.

1. Capitalize the first word of any direct quotation unless it is interrupted by, "he said," etc..

Examples

He questioned, "Are you leaving now?"

"Are you," he asked, "leaving now?"

2. Offset all quotations with either a comma, question mark, or exclamation mark.

Examples

"Why?" he asked.

"Now!" he demanded.

"Please bring them," he requested.

3. Use quotation marks to identify titles which are part of something bigger. Underline the main title (what would appear on the cover).

Examples

"To Build a Fire" is my favorite short story in the book,
The Short Stories of Jack London.
"I Want to Hold Your Hand" is an early Beatle song
on the CD, Meet the Beatles.

4. Use quotation marks to denote slang or to highlight words, phrases, or clauses that are identified in the sentence.

Examples

I think he lives in a "bad" house.
The word "dude" is overused by many.
The phrase "over the edge" is now standard English.

It is important to note and to teach students that in rules three and four, commas are not typically used to offset the quotation marks. The example regarding the Beatle CD is an appositive and therefore needs the comma.

Another aspect of quotations is the position of punctuation inside or outside the quotation marks. Here are the rules:

1. A period and comma are always placed inside of the closing quotes.

2. Question and exclamation marks are placed inside of the closing quotes in almost all occasions. The only exception is when the quote itself is not a question or exclaimed comment.

Example

Did you say, "You have to leave soon"?

82

We need to convince newspaper editors, advertisers, and fellow teachers that there is no such thing as a single quote unless it is contained inside of a double quote. This usage is so rare that until the sixth grade, most students do not need to even know a single quote exists.

The Colon

There is not a lot to say about teaching the colon; it is straightforward. There are a few little twists that are more linked to capitalization rules than those of the colon.

Use a colon to say, "And here they are..." It is almost as if the listeners are being prepared for an announcement.

Examples

Please send the following: paper, pens, and rulers.

His response was as follows: He bought a car, purchased three flares, and drove into a ditch.

He bought the following items:
1. Computer
2. Stereo components
3. Television

Note the capitalization rules here. If the items listed do not create a sentence, the items are not capitalized (first example). If the items listed create a complete sentence, the first letter after the colon must be capitalized (second example). If the items listed are in a list format (third example), always capitalize the first letter of each item.

A second use of the colon is after the salutation in a business letter (i.e., Dear Sirs:). The third use is in time (8:30).

I ask my students to minimize the use of the colon in their writing. It is a very strong punctuation mark and has a tendency to make student writing look and sound technical or instructional. It has a negative impact upon the flow of words.

Parentheses

This is another type of punctuation I ask students to use sparingly. The best use of parentheses is to create clarity in an awkward or confusing sentence. The major problem students have with parentheses is not in using them correctly, but in choosing the right placement for other punctuation when parentheses are added.

Basically, parentheses are used to offset unnecessary words, phrases, or clauses; numbers, letters or symbols used as appositives; or side comments to the reader.

Three basic rules to help students punctuate parentheses are:

1. Never use commas to offset parentheses.

2. If the parentheses begin and end a sentence, put the period inside the closing parenthesis.

3. If there are words in the sentence in addition to the words within the parentheses, always put the period outside the closing parenthesis.

He had four (4) different spellings for his name.
My uncle (the cheapest man I know) bought dinner for me.
Please return the attached brochure (see details on back).
She didn't want to attend. (I believe she made a mistake.)

The Dash

I happen to be enamored with the dash. Maybe it is the word, maybe the way it looks, or perhaps the freedom it represents. In one of the language books I consulted in writing this text, I chuckled when I read, "Excessive use of the dash indicates the writer does not know how to use other punctuation correctly." I am not certain I agree, but I do have to force myself to limit my writing to one dash per page. Fundamentally, a dash is used in three situations.

1. A dash can be used when the reader wants to expand upon or interrupt a comment.

Example
I was certain that Jim — in fact, every male in the room — felt a bit nervous about the speech.

2. A dash can also be used at the end of a sentence to clarify or restate a point.

Example
I wanted to help you begin, continue, and complete the project — your success was my goal.

3. A dash can also be used to to emphasize a point. This is very similar to an appositive.

Example

We let him participate in the game — one game — and he felt he should be the captain.

Underlining, Italics, and Boldface

With the advent of the computer, teachers are seeing some of the most highly embellished script in the history of mankind. I receive students' papers at the beginning of each year that have two or three different fonts, a variety of pitches (height), and a plethora of underlined, italicized, and boldfaced type.

I understand the fascination on the student's part, but we must convince them that font errors are as detrimental to an effective paper as are punctuation, spelling, and capitalization errors. The problem is that there is no universal protocol as to when these changes are appropriate.

Some possible generalizations are presented below; however, keep in mind that these are my personal rules. You will need to adjust to the conventions of your school and the grade level you teach.

1. Use only one traditional print-type font for the entire paper — no script, calligraphic, or casual fonts.

2. An acceptable pitch is 10 through 13.

3. Only use the underline for names of books, CD's, magazines, and other titles that would appear on a cover.

4. Never underline, boldface, or italicize the title of your paper.

5. Never mix underlining, italics, or boldface in any combination.

6. Never use italics or boldface within quotations, parenthesis, or dashes. Better yet, never use italics or boldface at any point in your paper.

When I present these conventions to my students, they are inclined to think I lack creativity and spontaneity. I respond that creativity comes in the words they write, not in the way they write their words. It is a point which needs continual repetition.

How demanding should we be regarding proper use of punctuation in students' writing? I believe we must call them on every mistake that is made which is inappropriate for that grade level. Given the following sentence, what corrections and point deductions are appropriate?

Example
While I was talking to my friend Billy the strange young man began to walk towards us and he called me by name.

Third and fourth graders should probably know that a comma is necessary before "and." Fifth graders should definitely place the comma before "and" and should probably add a comma after Billy. Sixth graders should definitely know both commas mentioned above.

Seventh and eighth graders should know to restructure the sentence. A comma before Billy would help with clarification but would make the comma after Billy seem awkward. If this sentence were written by one of my eighth grade students, I would suggest rewording.

We have to find the fine line in correcting punctuation. We cannot make so many corrections that students are overwhelmed, but we must make meticulous corrections that are appropriate for that student.

Capitalization

Learning capitalization seems like it should be easy. If it is a name, it is capitalized. If it is a common word, it should not be capitalized. This seems fairly black and white. Unfortunately, teaching capitalization can be very confusing. We need to simplify the way language texts teach this topic. For example, here is a listing of all of the items which should be capitalized according to a compilation of English books:

Names of particular persons	Names of particular places
Continents	Countries
States	Cities
Rivers	Mountains
Lakes	Falls
Harbors	Bays
Valleys	Definite regions
Localities	Political divisions
Bridges	Buildings
Monuments	Parks
Ships	Automobiles

Hotels	Forts
Dams	Railroads
Streets	Historical events
Historical periods	Historical documents
Governement bodies	Government departments
Political parties	Business organization
Fraternal Orgaizations	Clubs
Societies	Companies
Institutions	Titles of Rank
Days	Months
Holidays	Days of special observation
Sections of the country	Personified seasons
Names of celestial bodies	Titles of books
Song titles	Words referring to the Deity
The Bible	Books of the Bible
Sacred Books	I and O

In addition, there are several exceptions, including hyphenated words, family relations preceded by possessives, school subjects, certain words in titles, and adjectives derived from words with special meaning. Is it any wonder that students become confused by this plethora of information?

How can we simplify these fifty-four categories and numerous exceptions? I have developed a workable simplification.

Positive Rules (Capitalize)

Rule 1: Capitalize any word that would appear on a map.

Rule 2: Capitalize any word that would appear on a store-bought calendar.

Rule 3: Capitalize any word which would appear on a person's name tag at a meeting or family reunion.

Rule 4: Capitalize any word which would appear on the sign in front of a building.

Rule 5: Capitalize all words in a title except for articles, conjunctions, and prepositions.

Negative Rules (Do Not Capitalize)

Rule -1: Do not capitalize a school subject unless it is a language or numbered course (History 101).

Rule -2: Do not capitalize summer, winter, spring, fall, sun, moon, star, planet.

Rule -3: Do not capitalize names of family relations when they are preceded by a possessive pronoun.

Rule -4: Do not capitalize north, south, east, west or any combinations when they describe which way you are going. (Usually these are capitalized only after the word "the.")

Rule -5: Do not capitalize the word after a hyphen unless it is also follows a capitalization rule.

Over the past two years that I have taught this numbering method, my students' understanding of capitalization usage has improved significantly. Keep it simple and students can succeed.

There are few minor points to keep in mind. There are other words which are capitalized: the first word in a sentence, a listing of words in column form after a colon, the first word of a direct quotation, and all letters are capitalized in an acronym (MADD). All of these rules should be taught in conjunction with that type of punctuation.

Spelling and Usage

Of all that we teach, I believe that a successful spelling program — an approach in which students truly learn to spell words they do not already know and then remember them years later — is one of the most difficult.

The process used by many teachers of presenting a list of words, practicing them for a week, and then giving an oral spelling test on Friday can show short-term learning. In my experience, I do not see much in the way of long-term application.

There is no denying that learning to spell English is like trying to ride a cloud. How can one ever understand why proceed, precede, and supersede are spelled as they are. Similarly, the words you, through, ewe, who, new, shoe, glue, Pooh, and boo all end with the same sound. It is not too surprising that many students struggle with spelling.

There are rules which students can learn which will help them to spell more effectively. What I will share are a few of the mnemonics which I have developed to help students spell, and a proposed list of "never to be misspelled" words appropriate for each grade level.

Mnemonics in Spelling and Usage

An old adage we teach children is, "I before e, except after c or sounded as a as in neighbor and weigh — but there are exceptions." When I used to teach this, my students would understand the "after c" part and the "a in neighbor and weigh," but when the heard "exceptions" they would ask, "Then why learn the rule?"

I put together a saying that included most of the exceptions. "In leisure, seize neither nor their weird, foreign, ancient height either, and don't forfeit counterfeit protein or caffeine."

My students now memorize, "I before e, except after c or sounded as a as in neighbor and weigh, and the exceptions are: In leisure, seize neither nor their weird, foreign, ancient height either and don't forfeit counterfeit protein or caffeine."

Admittedly, this is a rather random list of words so I share the following story with my students....

Imagine you are sunbathing by a pool with a can of cola in your hand. Suddenly you look up and approaching you are two tall, exotic, yet beautiful/handsome women/men. They are quite a bit older than you, and you hear them speaking in an unknown language. Given this situation, you must remember, "In leisure, seize neither nor their weird, foreign, ancient height either, and don't forfeit counterfeit protein or caffeine."

Corny? Yes. Effective? In my experience, very. In fact, I have had students come back to visit years after graduation, and I ask what things they remember from class. A surprisingly high percentage remember these silly mnemonics they learned many years before.

A second phrase I teach my students are the words which end in "o" and require the addition of "cs" to form the plural. "A Negro hero's torpedo echo(ed) through the tomato and potato." The correct plural form spelling of these words is:

Negroes	heroes	torpedoes
echoes	tomatoes	potatoes

Compare these to words such as:

stereos	avocados	portfolios
shampoos	silos	ponchos

Some "o" words have optional spellings:

banjos or banjoes

cargos or cargoes

tornados or tornadoes

I do not worry about teaching students the optional words. As far as I am concerned, banjos, cargos, and tornados are acceptable. The saying, "A Negro hero's torpedo echo(ed) through the tomato and potato" provides all the help students need.

I use a similar approach with forming plurals of words which end with the "f" sound. Knife becomes knives, wife becomes wives, and shelf becomes shelves; however, chief becomes chiefs. There are but four exceptions, "The giraffe was safe with the chief sheriff." (Safe is being used as a verb, but the point is made to students that safe becomes safes.)

There are some words which can be written either way. Wharf can become wharfs or wharves, scarf can be scarfs or scarves, and hoof can be hoofs or hooves. Again, unless the word is giraffe, safe, chief, or sheriff, I want my students to keep it simple and write the plural word with a "v."

Homonyms can provide much confusion to students. It seems like we teach and reteach sets of words like to/too/two, their/their/they're, and it's/its until we are blue in the face. When we get a set of writing papers from students, inevitably they have misused (not misspelled) these words. I categorize these mistakes as "usage errors." I have included some of the techniques I use to teach these homonyms to students.

To/too/two: Students seem to be able to cope with the two spelling but get very confused with to/too. I explain that if the student can say "tuh" then the word should be spelled "to."

I am going tuh the store (to the store) [tuh sounds OK]
He is going tuh walk (to walk). [tuh sounds OK]
He is tuh tall (too tall). [because tuh does not sound right]
I'm going, tuh (too). [because tuh does not sound right]

Its/it's and whose/who's: It seems so easy to tell students that "it's" means it is, but it does not seem to register. The confusion for students is understandable when one considers that "its" and "whose" are possessive, but then we emphasize that when we write a possessive, we must add an apostrophe — Jim's or children's. They look at "it's" and "who's," and there is an apostrophe so it must be a possessive. It does not help that "it's" and "who's" follow a different apostrophe rule (to replace missing letters).

I teach students that the apostrophe in "it's" and "who's" is like the "dot" of an "i." When they write it's, the writer is replacing the "i" with a dot. One would not say, "It is paw was injured," so one would not write it's paw.

In the chapter on grammar, I suggest that you have students memorize the pronouns. Once students know, "my, your, his, her, its, our, their, whose," it is another way to remember the proper use of its and whose.

Their/there/they're: I keep experimenting with new ideas on these words. Currently, I explain to students that I

97

can **stay "here"** or **go "there."** They are like opposites. The word "here" can be found in "there."

"Their" is another one of those memorized possessive pronouns, but the next problem is spelling because it is also an exception to the ie/ei spelling rule. (It is any wonder students have difficulty sorting this out?) I start singing, "Old MacDonald and his wife had a farm, e-i-e-i-o," in class. They interrupt and comment that "and his wife" is not part of the song. I argue, "oh yes! And it was their farm; they own it! The e-i-e-i-o is just to help you remember how to spell it!" Then I write on the board "t-h-e-i-r farm."

Over the school year, whenever we review the word, I need only say, "Old MacDonald," or, "e-i-e-i-o," and the students get the point.

Once students learn "their" and "there," "they're" is the only spelling remaining. I find that getting them to say, "they are" to check for the "they're" usage takes practice but is not an overwhelming problem.

All ready/already/all right: I teach these together only because many students believe that "alright" is a word. It is not. It has recently become acceptable in informal cases but is still considered incorrect in formal writing. Whenever students want to write "all right," they must "write 'all' first." This technique is much harder to explain on paper than to say in class. Say the rule aloud, "If you want to write all right, you must write all first." This gets the idea across that "all" is a complete word and "right" comes after "all."

"All ready" means "completely prepared," and already means "previously." If students will substitute these synonyms, they can hear which is the proper word usage.

Weather/whether: My students continually make mistakes on this set of words. I think it is because they do not use the word "whether" very often so it does not completely register that there are two words that sound the same. I teach students to use "whether" when they are not certain whether it was he or her (she). Both "he" and "her" appear in the **whether**. Weather causes crops to grow so I tell them to be certain "eat" appears in "weather."

Past/passed: "Past" can be used as a noun, adjective, or adverb. "Passed" is a verb. I explain that "past" means "old days," "previous," or "by." If students can substitute old days, previous, or by in the sentence, always use past. If none of these work, use "passed."

Examples

noun adjective   adverb
In the past, past experiences have gone past me.
The train passed by.

Quit/quiet/quite: These are not homonyms, but they definitely cause a lot of confusion for students. If you quit your job, you cut it off or stop. Quit is the shortest (cut off) word.

For quite, I teach "quite white" which end with the same three letters. The mnemonic to remember quiet is becoming dated in that ET (the movie) is getting more and more obscure. ET, the character in the movie made very little noise; he was quiet. Therefore, qui-e-t.

Effect/affect: This is a very difficult set of words to teach. At times the actual meaning becomes almost interchangeable. I teach students that **effect means result**, and **affect means influence**. To help them remember, I point out the "e" in effect and result and then emphasize Effect is a REsult.

I used to teach that "effect" is a noun and "affect" is usually used as a verb, but I found this to be of almost no help to students as a sole means of determining which to use. Remember that verbs as verbals can function as nouns. It is too much to ask students in eighth or ninth grade to continually make this fine distinction without another guideline.

Students often comment that both "result" and "influence" sound correct in certain situations. For example, "The experiment had a negative influence/result." At this point, I refer students to the noun versus verb rule. In this case, it is obvious that what was negative is a noun; therefore, the word "effect" is correct.

Examples
My mother's input usually effects/affects my decisions.
(Results or influences? affects!)

The bomb had a devastating effect/affect.
(Result or influence? effect!)
I didn't think the song would have such an effect/affect.
(Result or influence? both work!) (Ask,"Is it being used as a noun?" yes, so the proper choice is "effect.")

Grade Level Word Lists

When we teach spelling, over the course of a year, students probably study between 500 and 1000 words. They should learn to spell them correctly and then use them properly in their writing. I believe there is a distinction between what a student should know and what he or she must know.

In my class, the student must know (memorize) the ten comma rules, the rules for using apostrophes, the prepositions, the linking verbs, and a myriad of other information I hammer home every day. I too present 500 or so spelling words, and students should know them. However, I also provide a list of words that students must know. These are referred to as "Rewrite Words." If a student misspells any of these words on a writing assignment, I stop correcting at that point, and he or she must rewrite the entire paper.

I am not including words like rhythm, psychology, or pneumonia. For an eighth grader, it is not too much to ask that he or she always spell words like "receive," "interest," and "separate" correctly. For a fourth grader, I believe it is reasonable to ask that words such as "right," "said," and "friend" always be spelled correctly.

We need to provide a list of words students are required to know. We must give them practice, and after repeated practice, they must always spell these words correctly.

The following lists represent a starting point. In your teaching situation, you will need to adjust these lists depending upon the level of your students. The ideal with this concept is to have your entire school adopt word lists. As a sixth grade teacher, your students would be responsible to never misspell any words on the fourth, fifth, or sixth grade lists.

When I grade papers, I still take points off for spelling if students misspell words that do not appear on these lists. They should know how to spell almost all of the words they write, but they must spell the rewrite words correctly, or rewrite their paper.

Fourth Grade Rewrite Words (introduced in third)

a lot	before	does	every
first	friend	how	once
right	said	talk	then
to	too	until	well
were	when	where	who
with			

Fifth Grade Rewrite Words (introduced in fourth)

about	again	always	are/our
because	didn't	doesn't	English
know	little	now	people
really	school	should	spelling
which	without	world	your
you're			

Sixth Grade Rewrite Words (introduced in fifth)

already	all right	answer	beautiful
college	describe	different	enough
example	explain	favorite	language
question	remember	sentence	surprise
there/their	though	thought	wouldn't

Seventh Grade Rewrite Words (introduced in sixth)

actually	another	corrected	finally
knowledge	literature	misspell	paragraph
science	signed	sincerely	supposed to
system	terrible	than	tomorrow
trouble	vocabulary	weather	whether

Eighth Grade Rewrite Words (introduced in seventh)

accurate	analyze	assignment	believe
business	cooperation	definite	difficult
difference	emphasis	experiment	information
interest	liquid	necessary	obvious
occasion	receive	recommend	separate

Ninth Grade Rewrite Words (introduced in eighth)

accept/except	angle	argument	belief
casual	committee	continuous	decision
edible	embarrass	exceed	naturally
neutral	opportunity	past/passed	proceed
relevant	succeed	successful	weird

The third grade does not have a list of rewrite words. In speaking with third grade teachers, the consensus is that while third graders practice spelling, the average student is at a very basic spelling level. They have not had enough consistent practice. To enforce a standard such as completing a rewrite due to misspelled words is not appropriate for this grade level.

Ninth graders do not have a new list introduced simply because by the time a student reaches high school, he or she should be spelling almost everything correctly. Since this is not always the case, the one hundred and twenty rewrite words from fourth through eighth grade provide an ample selection for those students who need remediation in spelling.

What I personally like about the instant rewrite words on a school-wide basis is that they provide a black and white criteria for students. Writing is subjective, and the rewrite words identify one tangible aspect of accountability on every paper students write.

The instant rewrite word for fourth grade should be posted on a wall chart in all fourth grade classrooms. The fourth and fifth grade instant rewrite lists should be posted in all fifth grade rooms. The fourth, fifth and sixth grade words should be posted in the sixth grade classrooms, etc. Given this approach, ninth graders will be looking at 120 words which should never be misspelled.

There are students who simply cannot spell. We can work with phonics, spelling games, syllabication, and a myriad of other techniques to very little long-term success. Their ability will improve, but they will never be proficient spellers. I am often asked about how the rewrite lists will affect these students.

In my classroom, I require all of my students to spell the rewrite words correctly. Some leeway is given to those who are severely poor spellers, but it is merely a sliver of freedom. I believe that given a list of twenty words to master (of course, the traditional spelling program continues as always), ninety-nine percent of students can write these words correctly on an assignment which they have had for a week or two.

At times, we let some students get away with being lazy. I can accept a student misspelling several words he or she has studied for only one week. I can forgive a student for misspelling words which he or she has never learned before. I cannot accept that any regular education student is unable to spell the words on the rewrite lists after intense instruction and practice.

If necessary, readjust, add, or simplify the essential spelling list. It is only a suggested list generated by teachers in our school.

I firmly believe that when your students start taking more responsibility to proofread and correct their errors, you will find they feel better about their writing. You will also spend less time in complete frustration as you correct their papers. Every mistake they do not make is fifteen seconds you save in correcting!

Yes, You Must Teach Grammar

Parts of speech, parts of a sentence, adverbial phrases, indirect objects, linking verb complements, and verbals are concepts that strike terror in the hearts of many teachers. We are supposed to know all of this "stuff," but guess what — we don't! We have developed a defense mechanism; the solution is, don't teach it.

The reason you do not know it is because the last generation of teachers were told to de-emphasize the structure of grammar so they did not teach it. It is time that we learned grammar because if we are going to talk the talk of writers, grammar is a necessary component.

You will not learn it all in a year; in fact, you will never learn it unless you make a true, concerted effort. My goal in this chapter is to demonstrate why you need to know grammar and give you some new and different ways to teach the concepts to your students.

Why do they need to know it?

Here are ten reasons why good writers must understand grammar. There are many more than ten, but hopefully, this will provide enough to convince you to learn as much as you can.

• Without understanding the nominative and objective cases, proper use of I/me, he/him, she/her, etc. is almost impossible.

• Without knowing the prepositions or identifying prepositional phrases, one cannot properly use the objective case pronouns. (It is obvious that sportscasters do not know this either.)

• Without understanding the difference between a subordinate (dependent) and independent clause, one cannot identify proper use of the comma when a conjunction connects the clauses.

• Without an understanding of possessive adjectives, the proper uses of its/it's and whose/who's are very difficult to learn.

• Without an understanding of the function of verbal and prepositional phrases, it is very difficult to properly use the comma to offset introductory phrases.

• Without a knowledge of helping verbs (auxiliaries), students will never understand the difference between active and passive voices.

• Without understanding linking verbs, students are destined to use adverbs rather than adjectives as complements.

• Without a knowledge of the difference between a coordinating conjunction and a subordinating conjunction, students cannot use semicolons properly.

• Without the ability to identify verbs and adjectives in their writing, communication with students becomes much more time consuming simply because you cannot quickly tell them how to enrich the vocabulary in their work.

• Without an understanding of the difference between a subordinate and independent clause, students can never differentiate simple, compound, and complex sentences.

A Crash Course in Grammar

I will share some of the fundamental ways in which I teach grammar to my junior high school students. This is not meant to be an all-inclusive grammar text. It shares the basics of what I believe students must know.

Parts of speech

Students often become confused between parts of speech and parts of a sentence. Make a clear distinction as part of your first grammar lesson. I suggest you display two wall charts. On one side of the front of the room, list the "Parts of Speech," on the other side, list "Parts of a Sentence." Making a clear delineation at the start will help your students differentiate between the two.

The parts of speech are nouns, verbs, adjectives, adverbs, pronouns, prepositions, conjunctions, and interjections. Students should memorize these as early as possible. N-V-A-A-P-P-C-I can be listed on the wall chart.

Nouns

The typical definition for nouns is, "a person, place, thing, or idea." I have found one of the best ways to have students identify a noun is to ask if they can say "the" in front of it and have it make sense. For example, the man (noun), the answer (noun), the quickly (not a noun). The most common exception is that "the" will not work before a proper noun (the Samantha, the Egypt).

There are basically five classifications of nouns. Students above grade six should know these. Every noun is either:

    singular or plural
    concrete or abstract
    masculine or feminine or neuter or both
    common or proper
    collective or non-collective

There are numerous creative ways to teach these in games, timed races, and memorization drills.

Verbs

Verbs are typically defined as words that can show action or a state of being. Personally, I have never had much success with the "state of being" definition. I find that students do identify verbs more effectively when I tell them that most verbs can have "ed" or "ing" added. This is actually a fairly accurate check.

There are three classifications of verbs — action, helping (also called auxiliary verbs), and linking verbs. To help students successfully identify these types, I have them memorize two of the sets.

Linking verbs connect a subject to a noun or adjective. I do not worry about teaching this to students at the beginning; I just want them to memorize the list of linking verbs:

am	is	are	was	were
be	been	being		
appear	become	feel	grow	look
sound	seem	smell	stay	taste	remain

Yes, English teachers, I am aware that all of these are not always used as linking verbs, but this is a very good place to start. The last two lines are in a rather random order, but there is reason for this listing as you will see. I use the following mnemonic device to help students remember the beginning letters:

111

A **Bee** Felt **Good** **Looking** (I tell students to imagine a bee staring into a mirror and combing his antennae).

Someone **Seemingly** **Smelled** **Stale** **Taco** **Remains** (I ask students to imagine a very unclean Mexican restaurant nearby).

As students are memorizing the verb list, I give them clues using these mnemonic sayings. It is bizarre, but you will be amazed how this information will stay with your students.

Helping or auxiliary verbs are the second classification of verbs. A helping verb always comes before another verb. If students have this list memorized, it is easy to identify them. There are no mnemonics here, just pure memorization:

am	is	are	was	were
be	been	being		
have	has	had		
do	does	did		
will	would	can	could	shall	should
may	might	must		
ought				

Action verbs are the third type and there are too many to memorize. Since students know all of the helping and linking verbs, there is no need memorize them. Obviously, if it is not a helping or linking verb, it must be an action verb.

Adjectives

Adjectives are "describing" words, but once again, this definition is quite confusing when one considers that: the, a, this, some, which, and my are all (at times) adjectives.

Over the years, I have perused many grammar texts, and it seems that in each, the number of types of adjectives increases. Years ago, I wrote a song which fits many tunes that can help students remember classifications of adjectives. I sing it to the tune of "School Days" by Chuck Berry.

The Adjective Song

An adjective describes a noun
There are eight types you've got to get down
Descriptive adjectives, there are a lot
Short, fat, skinny, and hot
Indefinite articles "an" and "a"
Definite "the" is all you say.

Demonstratives, there are four to know
This, that, these, and those.
Interrogatives are what, whose, and which.
Limiting have too many to list
But words like "all," "some," "any," or "few,"
"Several," "other" and numbers, too.

These are possessives so learn them too
My, your, his, her, its, our, their, whose
Proper adjectives you've got to try
American people, French fry
Comparatives: good, better, and best
Tall, taller, tallest and all the rest.

No, I do not believe the song writers of the world need fear my attempts, but I know my students can classify adjectives. We recite, sing, and dance to this song all of the time in class.

Adverbs

Adverbs describe (modify) verbs, adjectives, and other adverbs. When I tell students this, they stare blankly back at me. When I share that adverbs tell "time, place, manner, or intensity," they continue to stare.

I have found that the best way to explain adverbs is that they tell "when, where, how, and how much." That is, when it happened, where it happened, how it happened, and how strongly (or weakly) it happened. I also remind students that three-quarters of the adverbs they use will end in "ly."

One final point I teach is that if they see a word which does not seem to be any other part of speech, it is probably an adverb (i.e. yes, no, not, still).

Given these three explanations and a little bit of practice, students do pretty well with identifying most adverbs.

Pronouns

Pronouns are defined as words that take the place of a noun. The first day you present the concept of pronouns, begin with the phrase, "A pronoun is not a noun, and a noun is not a pronoun."

In order to teach pronouns effectively, I believe the students need to memorize lists. It is not enough to break these into personal, reflexive, and possessive (there are several other types of pronouns, but students who have learned the types of adjectives have also learned the other pronoun types — interrogative, limiting, and demonstrative). If students are to learn proper pronoun usage, they need to divide the personal pronouns into their cases.

This gets a bit technical, but it is important to teach this. There are three cases: nominative, objective, and possessive.

There are specific situations which require use of the nominative case pronoun: the subject of the sentence, a subject complement (after a linking verb), and an appositive referring to the subject of the sentence.

The objective case pronouns must be used as a direct object, indirect object, object of the preposition, and an appositive in any of these three cases.

The possessive case pronouns are the easiest to teach and are used universally to show possession.

I find it very beneficial for students to memorize these pronoun lists. Once memorized, determining proper usage is much easier.

nominative case pronouns: I, you, she, he, it, we, they,who*

objective case pronouns: me, you, him, her, it, us, them, whom*

possessive case pronouns: my, your, his, her, its, our, their, whose*

reflexive pronouns: myself, yourself, himself, herself, itself, ourselves, themselves

* note that I include the interrogative case "who, whom, whose"

115

Once students have these memorized, you will find that when you discuss parts of the sentence, much of it will become easier for them to grasp. When students learn that they must use an objective case pronoun only as a direct object, indirect object, and object of the preposition, the explanation of cases is valuable knowledge.

A second challenge in teaching pronouns is to have students differentiate between a pronoun and an adjective. They have a tendency to see, "This is mine," or "All were there," and automatically determine that "this" and "all" are adjectives. I have not found an easy way to explain this other than to remind students that they always must look to the next word to identify an adjective or pronoun. Even this approach is only about 90% accurate.

Prepositions

Prepositions are one of the most interesting parts of speech to teach. I tried one method after another and finally decided to write a poem to help student memorize the prepositions:

> aboard about above across
> against along around
> amid among after at
> except for during down
>
> behind below beneath beside
> between before beyond
> by in from off on over of
> until unto upon

under underneath since up
like near past throughout through
with within without instead
toward inside into to

I perform this poem in a variety of styles, from Shakespearean to Kermit the Frog, and have students memorize one verse per day. We play a variety of games to help them to learn it, and I continually test my students on this throughout the year. If you are not having your students memorize lists in your classroom, you are missing out on some enjoyable and challenging activities. Memorization for memorization's sake is pointless, but basic information to be drawn upon for application should be memorized.

Once students have prepositions memorized, they need only learn two more bits of information. First, a preposition must always be part of a phrase (group of words) and will always be the first word in the phrase — "inside the room," "above the sofa," etc. Second, if the preposition is not a part of a phrase, then it is an adverb. This is a difficult concept, but imagine how impossible it would be if students had to first figure out if the word "itself" were a preposition. Memorization solves this.

Conjunctions

Conjunctions are connecting words; the most common being: and, but, or, nor, for, yet. Students need to memorize this list to properly use comma rule four (use a comma before "and, but, or, nor, for, yet" when there is a complete sentence on either side).

A second type of conjunction is the correlative. These always come in pairs such as: either/or, neither/nor, not only/but also, etc. I don't spend much time with these.

The third type of conjunction does warrant attention: the subordinating conjunction. They are aptly named because they typically begin a subordinate (dependent) clause. A fairly complete list of subordinating conjunctions includes:

after	because	unless	although
before	since	until	as
even if	so as	when	even though
so that	whenever	as if	except
than	where	as long as	if
that	wherever	as soon as	in order that
till	whether	as though	provided
though	while		

Interjections

Interjections are the easiest part of speech to teach. They are simply words that are "thrown in" or "interjected" into writing or speech. With the proliferation of the student interjections, "like," "well," and "um," we have excellent models to identify each day in class.

Parts of a sentence

In my experience, it is best to teach all parts of speech before teaching parts of a sentence. Subjects, predicates, and objects are more abstract and have more exceptions. I begin with teaching the difference between a word, a phrase, and a clause.

A "word" I define as a group of letters that together have a meaning. Not that it is very important for anyone to know this, but at least it makes a distinction between a word and a phrase.

A phrase is a group of words that together act as one part of speech. Prepositional phrases are the easiest to teach and, until the sixth or seventh grade, are the only phrases students need to learn. Prepositional phrases function as either adjectives of adverbs.

If students are ever going to understand grammar, they need to understand the three types of verbals — infinitive (to + verb), gerund (verb + ing), and participial (verb + ing or ed [there are many irregulars]). Infinitives and gerunds are always used as nouns; participials are always adjectives.

A clause is a group of words that has a subject and a predicate; it may or may not be a complete sentence. There are two major categories of clauses: subordinate (dependent) and independent. Subordinate clauses can be used as adjectives or adverbs; independent clauses are simple sentences.

All of this discussion can get much more technical, but with grammar, we need to keep it as simple as possible.

The subject of a sentence becomes much more obvious to students once they can identify a noun and pronoun. The subject has various definitions depending upon what language book you are using. I like the definition, "who or what is doing something in the sentence." This definition leads smoothly into the definition of the predicate, "what the subject is doing."

In simple sentences, with practice, students can identify subjects and predicates fairly easily once they know the parts of speech. The problem is that if we want them to become effective writers, we must get them to write (and understand) compound, complex, and compound-complex sentences. Finding subjects and predicates in these sentences is much more difficult and takes a lot of practice.

Teaching direct and indirect objects causes many teachers to give up on grammar. It is at this point that most students start complaining, "Why do have to learn this?" My response is that without the knowledge of objective cases, one will never know when to properly use pronouns, and will never be able to learn a foreign language properly.

If students can identify a subject and predicate, they can find a direct object. It simply answers, "what or whom the subject and predicate are talking about." One basic rule to teach students about direct objects is that not every sentence has a direct object.

Indirect objects add more confusion to the mix. The three rules to teach student are:

1. You cannot have an indirect object unless there is a direct object.

2. An indirect object will always come before a direct object.

3. An indirect object will never be part of a prepositional phrase.

An indirect object is defined as, "to what or to whom the direct object is directed." The essential concept in having student understand indirect objects is to be certain they can identify prepositional phrases.

In the sentence, "He gave the book to me," "me" is an object of the preposition, not an indirect object. If the sentence were, "He gave me the book," then "me" becomes an indirect object. This is a very confusing concept for the students to grasp.

Objective complements (also called linking verb complements) are nouns, pronouns, or adjectives which are found after a linking verb (students memorize these). "It is Ben," "She seemed happy," or, "It was I," are samples of sentences with objective complements.

The critical distinction here is that simply because a linking verb is used, there may or may not be an objective complement. The word following the verb is only a complement if it links or modifies the subject.

A teacher who wishes to take his or her students to the next level of grammar embarks upon a perilous task. The adjectival and adverbial clause, restrictive versus non-restrictive clauses, the structure and position of the noun clause, absolute construction, and transitive and intransitive verbs are beyond the scope of many non-college bound students.

The information I present in this chapter is, in my opinion, essential information for every student. To know parts of speech, parts of the sentence, and the various classifications of each is fundamental. Those items mentioned in the previous paragraph warrant instruction, but the audience is a select group.

I believe we must teach grammar to enable students to improve their writing. As a teacher, I want to know all I can about grammar, but when it comes to my students, I am very satisfied if they can master the basics that I present here.

Vocabulary

Since this is a book about teaching writing, I would be remiss not to include discussion about vocabulary. There is no trick to teaching vocabulary to students, the trick is in motivating students to remember and use what they learn.

In terms of vocabulary in student writing, there are three basic points which I emphasize: Be certain the word fits, beware of repetition, and be selective of which words are chosen to be replaced with more sophisticated words.

I am certain many teachers have had to find a remedy for a student disease which I refer to as "thesaurusitis." The opening stage of this affliction is a paper in which the student has used static, dull, uninteresting words.

Example
He went up the stairs and saw his brother. His brother was just waking up and looked tired and sleepy. He said, "Hurry up and get dressed. Let's go to the game today."

The teacher's comments on the student's work might be, "You must try to use more interesting words." On the next writing assignment, the student, in hopes of pleasing his teacher, consults the thesaurus for more dynamic words and writes:

He bounded up the parapet and envisioned his sibling. His brother was just arising and appeared fatigued and slumbering. He retorted, "Hurry up and outfit yourself. Let's attend the competition today."

The student is now experiencing stage two thesaurusitis, and we teachers have to explain the concept of "middle ground."

I have discovered that this scenario needs to be played out with many students each year. They are accustomed to writing dull passages, and when they are encouraged to add spice, they overdo it.

There are two models which I present to help cure the curse of thesaurusitis. My first approach is to explain the concept of intensity of words. On the board, I randomly write a set of words such as: happy, pleased, enchanted, ecstatic, enthusiastic, smiling, content. I then ask students which of these words are the most and least intense. Typically, they will choose ecstatic and pleased. I then ask them to arrange the remainder of the words in a hierarchy of intensity.

Over the next week or two, a daily activity or home-work assignment is to develop a list of five to ten synonymous words listed in order of intensity. For many students this is an interesting discovery.

My second approach is to have students imagine a wide, flat board with a small groove notched down the center. I even draw a representation on the chalkboard.

I explain that in every situation in writing, there is one word which fits perfectly in the groove. Some of the words in the list of intensity will be too strong for a given situation, and some will be too weak. Their challenge as writers is to find the word that fits in the groove perfectly. The most intense word will work sometimes, and the most inexpressive word will work at other times. In general, however, it is one of those "in-between" words that will "fit the groove."

In writing, choosing just the right word can be the difference between mediocrity and excellence or between mundane and sophisticated. Think of the effect of the words yell versus chastise; look versus glance; touch versus caress; or trudge, tramp, or sludge versus walk. The more dramatic word in each set is obvious.

Another important consideration in teaching vocabulary is the elimination of repetition. There is nothing that makes writing more static than overuse of the same word or phrase. The rules I teach regarding repetition include:

1. Never begin two consecutive sentences with the same word or phrase (better yet, avoid beginning any two sentences in a paragraph with the same word or phrase).

2. Never end a sentence and begin the next sentence with the same word or phrase.

Example

He went up the stairs and saw his brother. His brother was just waking up and looked tired and sleepy.

3. Never repeat a very descriptive or intense word within a paragraph, and never repeat a highly descriptive or intense word in the same essay.

Examples

He was preoccupied by all that had occurred. (descriptive)
He infiltrated the rebel group. (very descriptive)
The attorney badgered the witness. (highly descriptive)

4. Try to avoid repeating any word within the same sentence unless you are using this as a technique of "driving the nail." This is my term to describe repeating a word several times to make a specific point. It is an excellent technique but must be used sparingly.

Examples

He went shopping and bought a lamp, bought a CD, and bought a new tape player.

If you're going to be a success in life you must work long and hard, work to your maximum ability, and work without complaint.

No matter how hard I tried to please my father, it was never good enough, never fast enough, and never appreciated in any way.

The first example is a very weak use of driving the nail. The second example is better, but the topic is not quite strong enough to warrant this emphasis. The third sentence is more emotional, and one can imagine a young person saying it this way out of frustration with the intent of "driving" the point home for the reader.

Rewritten Examples
He went shopping and bought a lamp, a CD, and tape player.

If you're going to be a success in life you must work long and hard, perform at your maximum ability, and persevere without complaint.

The rewritten examples are the types of suggestions I would make to students to help them avoid repetitive words.

The third aspect of teaching vocabulary is to help students to identify which words need to be geared up to a higher (or lower) intensity. When students finish writing a sample paragraph in class, I would suggest they scan the paper and identify all of the verbs and adjectives. The problem with this suggestion for many teachers is that students do not know how to identify a verb or an adjective?

If your students are at this fundamental level, they need daily practice to become not only able, but skilled at finding specific parts of speech in their writing. To give students practice, I begin by collecting a set of student-generated paragraphs, and I cover their names with white labels. I then make overhead transparencies of the most legible papers. Each day in class, I display one of the overheads and together we identify the verbs and adjectives (in so doing we also identify other parts of speech).

Students then select the weakest verb(s) and adjective(s) and try to step them up to a higher level. I believe they need only change two verbs or two adjectives to greatly improve the sound of each paragraph. If they try to change all of the words, a minor case of thesaurusitis occurs. In this process, I continue to remind them to make the new word fit in the groove.

Addressing these three vocabulary concepts has worked well for me. It is an ongoing process, but with specific activities to focus students, enhancing vocabulary is one of the more readily accomplished aspects in helping students to write more effectively.

One final point which might be considered: Where should the vocabulary words come from? My philosophy has always been to link two writing assignments (this is discussed thoroughly in the year-long planning chapter). I try to provide a list of twenty-four to thirty vocabulary words for each set of writing assignments. For an elementary school teacher, the topics of these assignments can be related to the students social studies, science, and literature units. I suggest trying to select words from these subject areas to create their vocabulary lists.

If students learn definitions and then have the opportunity to write the words in their extended writing assignments, they tend to learn the meanings and usages more completely.

This is a much more effective approach than teaching lists of words from a vocabulary book which has no link to the writing which students are doing in class. We learn (and teach) vocabulary with the intent of using the words to enhance our ability to express ourselves. Using new vocabulary in writing is the best way to accomplish this goal.

Sentence Structure

A fundamental element in good writing is a flow of sentences. It is so easy to say and so difficult to teach. When sentences work together, there is a rhythm or cadence with allows the reader to settle in and enjoy. On the other hand, when sentence structure is weak, it is almost impossible to get comfortable with the writing. To me, it is as though I am being poked, needled, or read to in a voice full of static.

Identifying what makes one group of sentences work and another set of sentences less pleasing is the next goal.

Types of Sentences

Sentences are categorized in two different ways. First, they can be identified as declarative, interrogative, imperative, and exclamatory. Second, they can be separated into types of clause combinations which include: simple, compound, complex, and compound-complex.

The declarative, interrogative, imperative, and exclamatory sentences are usually taught in the younger grades (second and third) in conjunction with teaching ending punctuation. A period is used at the end of declarative sentences, a question mark with interrogative, and an exclamation with exclamatory. Either periods or exclamation marks can be used with imperative sentences. By fifth or sixth grade, these rules of punctuation are generally mastered.

The second grouping of sentences is more a categorization of clause combinations. The simple sentence contains one independent clause; a compound sentence consists of two or more independent clauses. A complex sentence is one independent clause and at least one dependent (subordinate) clause. A compound-complex sentence is two independent clauses and at least one dependent clause.

It might seem surprising that the latter of the two groups described above is identified using the word "clause." In reality, sentences are merely combinations of the two types of clauses — independent and subordinate. This simplistic approach makes teaching simple, compound, complex, and compound-complex sentences much easier.

The how and why of teaching sentence/clause structure.

I believe we should introduce the term "clause" when we begin teaching students about sentences. They are synonymous, and by introducing the "clause" and "sentence" together, we eliminate the confusion of adding a new term at a later time.

When the topic of the sentence (clause) is first introduced in the first or second grade, teachers usually explain that a sentence is a complete thought. Typically, the words "subject" and "predicate" are not introduced. Students usually begin to write sentences using the way in which they talk as a model. Second grade teachers do have to deal with the concept of run-on sentences, but the actual structure or grammatical construction of the sentence is introduced in third grade.

As the terms "subject" and "predicate" become part of the vernacular, students often get mixed up deciphering between the "subject and predicate" and "nouns and verbs." After all, they are similar (to a point). If the teacher is clear in his or her mind as to the difference between parts of a sentence and parts of speech, the differentiation is not hard to teach. My experience is that many of us are a bit "uncertain" when it comes to grammar so we teach this information without a sense of commitment and comfort. The students are turned off to grammar because it seems nebulous.

There are situations where students have had excellent grammar instruction in the third and fourth grades, and the fifth grade teacher, not feeling comfortable with expanding the grammar curriculum, ignores it, and students forget much of what had been learned.

My experience tells me that the majority of students cannot become effective writers unless they understand grammar. They cannot write smooth sentences unless they understand how sentences work. We cannot specifically communicate with them as to how they can improve if they do not understand the basic structure of the sentence.

133

I like cars. Cars are fun to ride in. I never drove a car. I will drive when I get older. My brother has a neat car. He drives fast. My dad has a car too. He drives slow. I can hardly wait till I can drive.

If you were correcting this paper, how would you explain to the student what changes in the sentence structure needed to be made? Perhaps, "Your sentences are too short and choppy. Try combining some of them using 'and' or 'but.'"

Example

I like cars and cars are fun to ride in. I never drove a car. I will drive when I get older, but my brother has a neat car. He drives fast, and my dad has a car too, and he drives slow. I can hardly wait till I can drive.

If the student understands the concept of a simple sentence, can identify the subjects and predicates, understands that a subordinate clause begins with transition words like "when" or "since," and knows that a compound sentence needs a comma before and, but, or, nor, for, yet, your comments can be very specific. "You have written nine sentences and only about forty-five words. When you rewrite, use least eight words per sentence. To do this you will need to combine some into compound sentences. Also, in your paragraph, every sentence begins with a simple subject. Use some transition words (i.e. since, while, or as) to begin sentences. You used 'I' six times, eliminate two of them."

Example

I like cars and cars are fun to ride in. Though I never drove a car, I will drive when I am older. My brother has a neat car, and he drives fast. My dad has a car too, but he drives slow. I am excited about when it is my turn to drive.

When the teacher can converse with the student and give specific suggestions such as, "Use at least eight words per sentence, use some compound sentences, begin some sentences with transition words, and use 'I' four times." The student can work at writing as though it is a puzzle. He or she has all of the pieces. This is why we must teach grammar and sentence structure.

There are a number of interesting ways to begin teaching our students about clauses and sentences. Whether you have third graders who do not have clue about the terminology of the sentence, or you are working with ninth graders who have been taught the concept six times but still do not get the idea, these lesson ideas are appropriate.

Add It, Change It

This method be used in a game-type format or as a structured lesson. The goal is to link the concept of noun and verb to subject and predicate. We then add words to create different types of sentences.

One of my favorite concepts in education is the "critical attribute." It is the unique feature of a bit of information that makes that concept different from any other.

For example, the critical attribute of a preposition is that it is a word that tells position or location but must be a part of a phrase. There is no other word that does this. An adverb can tell location, but it need not be part of a phrase. The critical attribute of information generates a rule that is constant and true only to that information. The more we can identify the critical attributes of concepts and share these with our students, the more thoroughly they will learn what we are teaching.

Begin by asking students for a noun, for example, "Herman," and write this word on the board. For younger students, re-explain the concept of a noun — person, place, thing, or idea. Now, ask for a verb that fits with the noun, i.e., "walks." Write this on the board as well.

Explain to students that "Herman" is a noun and "walks" is a verb, but when they are written together, they form an independent clause. This is also called a simple sentence. If a noun and verb successfully work together, they add to their identities. The noun also becomes a subject, and the verb becomes a predicate. The critical attribute here is that in order for a noun and verb to become a subject and predicate, they must work together to explain something.

Ask students for another noun which is not capitalized, "parents." Elicit another verb, "talk." Put them together and another independent clause or simple sentence is formed, "Parents talk." Review the concept that "parents" is still a noun but has also become a subject. "Talk" is still a verb but is also a predicate.

It is imperative that the concept of noun/verb and subject/predicate be taught together. Without the identification of the critical attribute, most of the students linger in a never-land of grammar-dumb; that is, grammar does not make sense, and it is dumb.

"Add It, Change It" is not a one day lesson; it is ongoing and can generate a myriad of offshoots and permutations.

Once students comprehend the concept of subject-predicate, the teacher can begin explaining the compound sentence. By simply placing a conjunction between the two student-generated sentences, a compound sentence has been created: "Herman walks and parents talk."

When you begin teaching the compound sentence, it is important to identify the different applications of the word "compound." To help students identify the difference, ask students for two nouns, "Herman and Bertha." Ask students for a verb, "walk." Write the sentence, "Herman and Bertha walk" on the board. Explain that the nouns have now become subjects because they are working with a verb to make sense. But because there are two nouns, we have created a compound subject.

To emphasize the concept, ask students for a noun, "parents," and ask for two verbs, "talk and listen." Write the sentence on the board, "Parents talk and listen." The noun "parents" is now a subject, and the verbs "talk" and "listen" create a compound predicate.

Ask if it is possible to have a compound predicate and a compound subject, "Herman and Bertha walk and talk." Question if there could a compound subject and a compound predicate in a compound sentence, "Herman and

Bertha walk and talk, and parents and grandparents talk and listen."

Using this procedure we are leading students through all of the terminology and all of the overlaps and pitfalls. This is how we must teach these concepts. Do not hold anything back. Show students that "compound" always means that something is "doubled," that the subject and noun are related, as are the verb and predicate. When we teach the critical attribute, it all begins to make sense to the students (and to us).

Where can "Add It, Change It" go from here? The opportunities are endless, but the approach can also help explain the subordinate (dependent) clause.

To teach the meaning of subordinate, ask where a "sub" navigates, "**under** water." "For whom does a 'sub' teacher work?" **under** the supervision of the regular teacher. The prefix "sub" means **under** or **less than**. A subordinate clause is like an independent clause. It has a subject and predicate, but it is less than that. It cannot stand alone; it must be connected to an independent clause in order to be a sentence.

You can make the same distinction if you are teaching the term, "dependent" clause. Small children depend on their parents, and flowers depend on rain for survival. Children and flowers cannot stand alone; they need something else to be complete.

When students have a basic understanding of the words "subordinate" and "dependent," again ask students for a simple two-word sentence, "Herman walks." This is usually where I put a game into action. Dividing the class into two teams, I ask one student on one team to add a word to the clause/sentence. I caution, however, that the word must make sense with the subject and predicate.

One student responds, "quickly." Write, "Herman walks quickly," and ask if this is still a complete sentence. Explain that this is all we do when we write sentences — we add words to the subject and predicate.

Chose a student on the other team to supply another word, "weird." Write, "Weird Herman walks quickly." Return to a different student from the first team to supply a word, "away." "Weird Herman walks quickly away." At this point, other than adding a string of descriptive adjectives, there are not many choices for single words. There is one classification of words that when added, changes the sentence from an independent clause (simple sentence) to a subordinate clause (an incomplete sentence).

Let students struggle for an answer and eventually, someone will volunteer a word such as "while," "since," "because," or "when." Add this to the sentence on the board, "While weird Herman walks away quickly," and ask if there is a problem. With this one moment of teaching, the concept of the subordinate clause comes clear to most students.

To begin the next lesson, write a compound sentence on the board and add one of the transition words to the first clause. In so doing, you have created a complex sentence. From this model, one can explain proper use of commas and describe the difference between a compound and complex sentence.

You can use the same approach to teach that a phrase is a group of words that function as a single part of speech. Students cannot always add just one word to the models written on the board and have the sentence make sense. They may have to add something like, "down the street." Since "down the street" tells where something happened, it is a group of words (a phrase) that functions as an adverb.

For older students, you can play this game to teach direct and indirect objects. There are a number of other applications.

"Add It, Change It" is an ideal method to unlock the mystique of the clause. Use it with your third graders or your high school freshmen. All of a sudden, the structure of the sentence will make sense. The benefit is that when you correct student writing, you will be able to write comments which give them the specific direction they need to improve their writing.

Skeleton

At times, I find the best way for students to learn how to do a task the right way is to model doing it incorrectly. In writing, this would mean taking a well-written paragraph and extracting all the subjects, predicates and objects to make the paragraph sound basic and immature.

The following is an example of a paragraph which was presented in a previous chapter and has been "skeleton-ized."

Example

It seemed at all we did was drive, and each time we stopped it was to visit another historical site. That morning in Washington D.C. was different. We stepped out of our hotel and walked four or five blocks. Suddenly, I was amazed by all that surrounded me, the Capitol building off the distance, the White House to my left, a vast field of grass and two ponds reflecting a towering white monument. "What's that?" I asked my dad, and he responded, "That's the Washington monument, in memory of George Washington." "A monument, a city named in his honor, this must be someone who made a difference," I though to myself. As I began to learn more about his courage, his leadership, and his patriotism, I realized he had indeed accomplished much.

"Skeletonized" Example

All we did was drive, and we stopped. Morning was different. We walked blocks. I was amazed. "What is that?" I asked. He responded, "The monument." This must be someone. I began to learn more. He had accomplished much.

An alternative approach to skeleton is to give students the basic paragraph and have them add words or phrases to make the paragraph more interesting. Regardless of the approach you take, you will need to model this several times before students can do this successfully.

I have found the trick is to make it a game. When students simplify, have them read their samples in a tone of voice that mocks this basic style of writing. If students play with these concepts rather than being force-fed, their entire outlook on grammar and writing becomes more positive.

Earlier in this chapter, I used an example of a poorly-written paragraph and included two sets of sample teacher comments. I hope, after reading this chapter, I have convinced you that teaching the grammatical aspect of sentence structure is absolutely essential. Let us take a look at another sample to see if all of this makes more sense.

Example

My mom, Helen, is a wonderful person. She helps me out in many ways. Each morning she makes breakfast, and at night, she makes dinner, and she sometimes brings my lunch to me at school. My dad works real hard so mom has to do most of the chasing around to pick me up after school and after basketball practice and my brother when he finishes playing football. She never complains and sometimes we're not as nice to her as we should be. She is a nice person.

My comments on the paragraph would be, "I like the way you have described your mom; it definitely sounds like you respect and love each other. It is nice to read that. You need to work on rewording some sentences. You have six sentences that range from 5 to 33 words. Rewrite these in six or seven sentences, but each must have at least ten words and no more than twenty. Don't use 'and' more than once in any sentence."

Example

My mom, Helen, is a wonderful person, and she helps me out in many ways. Everyday she makes breakfast, dinner, and my lunch for school. My dad works real hard so mom has to do most of the chasing around. She picks me up after school, after basketball practice, and gets my brother when he finishes playing football. She is such a nice person, and she never complains. Sometimes we're not as nice to her as we should be, but I think she still knows we love her.

Granted, every student is not going to be this successful in piecing the puzzle parts together, but this student's first example was fairly good; therefore, he or she probably would have the ability to apply the suggestions I made.

The most interesting aspect of this approach is that at first, students grumble and moan about the work involved to count, reword, and restructure. This attitude changes when they read their final product. Suddenly, their work sounds more sophisticated, and they begin to feel like writers.

Verb Tense

This information probably could be covered elsewhere in this book, but it is such a pet peeve of mine that I felt compelled to designate a short chapter on verb tense.

My advice can be summed up in two words, "past tense." I continually tell my students that when telling a story, they must write in the past tense. Consider these examples.

Example in Present Tense

I walk to up to the Statue of Liberty and look up. I am amazed at the immense size and power of this statue. I wait in line, and with my dad, I walk up the stairs. It is cold and dark with only a dim light every ten to twenty yards. We climb and eventually reach the top. I gaze out at the huge skyscrapers of New York City. I see the blue water of the harbor turn white as boats churn along their way. I realize it is time to walk down those hundreds of steps. I stop to let my dad's knee rest — it always hurts when he walks down stairs. We eventually reach the bottom, and I realize I too am tired. It is a good day, and I board the boat to return to the mainland.

Example in Past Tense

I walked to up to the Statue of Liberty and looked up. I was amazed at the immense size and power of this statue. I waited in line, and with my dad, walked up the stairs. It was cold and dark with only a dim light every ten to twenty yards. We climbed and eventually reached the top. I gazed out at the huge skyscrapers of New York City. I saw the blue water of the harbor turn white as boats churned along their way. I realized it was time to walk down those hundreds of steps. I stopped to let my dad's knee rest — it always hurts when he walks down stairs. We eventually reached the bottom, and I realized I too was tired. It was a good day, and I boarded the boat to return to the mainland.

When reading through these two examples, I am amazed at how differently they affect me. The first, written in present tense, has no impact at all. I keep thinking, "How could all of this happen at the same time?" When I read the second, a sense of recollection enhances the passage. It is not that the writing is exemplary; rather, the verb tense lets me know that this is not all happening at once. It sounds better.

There is one phrase in present tense, "...it always hurts when he walks down stairs." This is appropriate because it is a thought, or an aside, that the writer conjures as he is writing; it is not part of the story.

While I stress the use of the past tense, there are many times when present tense works perfectly well. If you look at the examples in the chapter on Opening and Closing Paragraphs, many are written in the present tense and are very readable; however, whenever one writes a narrative or describes a personal anecdote, insist that students use past tense verbs.

A second issue concerning verb tense is students who shift between present and past tense. This is an obvious error to the reader, but some students have difficulty in being consistent.

A third verb problem many students must overcome is use of the passive rather than active voice. The passive voice is two verbs used together, a helping (auxiliary) plus an action verb. Note the difference between these two passages:

Example in Passive Voice

I had been walking for hours and had decided to stop and rest for awhile. Looking around me, I was surprised to see dark grey clouds were hovering above me. I was worried, and I was certain concern was showing on my face. I was carrying no rain gear and my tent, that once had been waterproof, had lost its abilty to shed water and was now absorbing more water than it was repelling. I might have been overreacting, and I did prepare for the worst. An hour later, my worst fears were proven true. Rain was pouring from the sky, and I was shivering and cold for the remainder of the night.

Example in Active Voice

I walked for hours and decided to stop and rest for awhile. Looking around me, I was surprised to see dark grey clouds hovering above me. Worry and concern showed on my face. I carried no rain gear, and my tent, that was once waterproof, had lost its ability to shed water and now absorbed more water than it repelled. I probably overreacted, but I prepared for the worst. An hour later, my worst fears proved true. Rain poured from the sky, and I shivered with cold for the remainder of the night.

147

In the preceding chapter on grammar, I listed the helping verbs and recommended that you have your students memorize them. When students know the auxiliaries, finding them in their writing is simple. It is another application in which learning grammar helps students to be more successful writers.

A final consideration regarding verbs is the overuse of the forms of "to be." "Am, is, are, was, and were" are five verbs that can overwhelm a reader. In descriptive writing, subject complements (linking verb complements) are used extensively. "It was breathtaking," "they were disbelievers," "we are inspired" are samples of this type of construction.

In descriptive writing, have students introduce other linking verbs as substitutes for forms of "to be." A "was" here and a "were" there are much easier to digest if the student uses words like "appeared," "seemed," "looked," "became," or "remained" as alternates. The list of linking verbs appears on page 111.

Verbs and adjectives are the two parts of speech that can make writing come alive. Before students worry about the most dramatic verb to use, they must first be able to use verbs in a consistent tense. Hopefully, that will most often be past tense.

A Hierarchy of Writing Skills

Throughout this book, I have continually alluded to the specifics of writing. I believe there is a hierarchy of skills that is incremental. The goal paper identifies these specifics, and if we want our students to attain mastery, we must clearly define the steps which will allow them to achieve this goal.

I wanted to keep these steps as concise and easy to follow as possible, yet when we talk about writing, there are so many components that "concise" and "easy to follow" are challenging accomplishments. The task analysis (hierarchy of skills) is presented grade by grade (with specific notes pertaining to special considerations and extenuating circumstances).

These are not objectives created and agreed upon by thousands of professors and teachers in a nationwide collaborative effort; rather, they are mine. They were created by one person and based upon personal experience.

I invite you to challenge them, pick them apart, move them around, and ignore those you dislike. In all of my years in education, I have never seen a task analysis like this. I believe that is the very reason that teaching writing has such mystique and confusion. The goal is to get you thinking about the measurable specifics of a writing program.

When we correct a student's paper, there are numerous ingredients that, when integrated, make an essay or story work well. These are:

I. Mechanics
   1. Spelling (Sp)*
   2. Punctuation (Punc)
   3. Usage (Use)
   4. Capitalization (Cap)
II. Organization
   1. Opening paragraph (OP)
   2. Thesis (Thesis)
   3. Paragraphing (Pgph)
   4. Closing or summary paragraph (CP)
   5. Overall appearance and neatness (Neat)
   6. Format of paper (Fmt)
III. Internal structure
   1. Sentence structure (SS)
   2. Vocabulary (V)
   3. Transitions (T)
   4. Verb tense (VT)
   5. Point of view (POV)
IV. Creativity
   1. New ideas (Ideas)
   2. Personal style (Prs)

* Abbreviations as they appear in the task analysis are in parentheses.

In the following task analysis of skills, the goal is to demonstrate that each grade level has an important part in bringing the student to a certain level of writing proficiency. If third graders can visualize and always write in multiple paragraphs, fourth graders can begin to organize them more completely, fifth graders can put richer ideas into the structure while sixth graders begin to develop their own styles. Junior high students are more able to put all of this together with dramatic vocabulary, interesting sentence structure and unique approaches. If we all do our own small part, it takes the pressure off of each teacher to attempt to do it all.

It would be absurd to believe that every student will attain all levels of success at each grade level. It is just as ridiculous to imagine that students are not going to stretch into the next grade level's skills. There are fourth graders who are working in the seventh/eighth grade hierarchy just as there are ninth graders who are somewhere between the fifth and sixth grade.

The purpose of this task analysis is to lessen the pressure on the teacher in terms of teaching writing. Until a student has mastered the third grade skills, there is no point in hammering on the fourth or fifth grade skills. They are beyond the level of comprehension or sophistication.

I also believe a student must write a least three to five papers which demonstrate awareness and application of a skill before we can acknowledge that it is mastered.

What we are trying to develop here is habits. This is the reason that I believe we must have students write an extended paper every two weeks. They need lots of practice before a habit is developed. However, as one will see from viewing this task analysis, the amount we must correct or the type of corrections we make on each paper is based on that student's level of ability.

The skills for each grade level are presented in two different forms. The first is from the teacher's perspective; that is, what is wrong with the writing. They are the first half of the comments which might appear on a student's paper.

The second half of this input must be generated by the teacher to make the correction measurable. For example, "Your essay is only one paragraph in length. On your next paper, you must write at least three paragraphs; one to introduce the topic, the second to describe the topic, and the third to close the essay. Listen closely in class when we discuss this organization."

You will also notice that in within each grade level's objectives, there is a list of spelling words (Sp) and rewrite words (RW). The spelling words presented in the third grade become the rewrite words in the fourth grade. (A complete discussion of the rewrite words is presented on pages 101 through 104.)

Clearly, students in third grade will study many more spelling words than those listed. The purpose of identifying these words on the task analysis is to let students know that these are fundamental spelling words that must always be spelled correctly. If in fourth grade, any of these words are misspelled, a rewrite or some type of major point reduction will take place.

The rewrite words are collective; that is, the twenty or so fourth grade rewrite words will add to twenty new words in fifth grade. Fifth graders will then have forty "rewrite words." By the time students are in ninth grade, they will have one hundred and twenty rewrite words.

The words listed under spelling words (Sp) at each grade level should be practiced continually at that grade level because they become rewrite words the following year.

Third Grade

Neat	Handwriting is illegible.
Fmt	Essay is only one paragraph in length.
Neat	Does not write to margin lines.
Pgph	Entire essay is only ten to fifteen lines in length.
SS	Paragraph is all one sentence, or there are continuous run-on sentences.
Cap	No title or title is not capitalized.
Cap	No words are capitalized.

Sp			
	a lot	before	does
	every	first	friend
	how	off	once
	right	said	talk
	then	to	until
	want	well	were
	when	where	who
	with		

Third graders are just beginning to understand that there is power in words. Cliques and inappropriate language begin to filter into the students' repertoire. Criticizing a classmate or adding an expletive to a conversation creates a stir among the group. This is indeed power.

For the first time, students can make sense of putting paragraphs and complete thoughts together. The third grade papers that I have read generally work best if they are three paragraphs in length. Each paragraph is three to six sentences and is fairly basic.

The writing skills to develop in third grade are more format oriented. From a grammatical standpoint, the structure of the sentence, identifying nouns and verbs, subjects and predicates, learning basic applications on commas, applying ending punctuation marks, and developing the structure of a paragraph are realistic third grade goals.

Fourth Grade

OP	There is no opening paragraph; no attempt to create interest.
CP	There is no closing paragraph.
Fmt	Leaves blank lines between paragraphs or does not indent.
Fmt	Writes "The End" at the end or uses some other "yearbook" closing.
SS	Sentences overuse "and," "because," and other connecting word.
Voc	The title and first words of essay are the same.
OP	The opening paragraph is the whole essay — the remainder repeats.
CP	Closing paragraph is one sentence.

RW			
	a lot	before	does
	every	first	friend
	how	off	once
	right	said	talk

154

	then	to	until
	want	well	were
	when	where	who
	with		
Sp	about	again	always
	are/our	because	didn't
	doesn't	English	know/now
	little	people	really
	school	should	spelling
	too	which	without
	world	your	you're

The students who are going to be natural writers begin to shine in the fourth grade. Unfortunately, there are a number of fourth graders who are still trying to master third grade skills so the range of abilities can seem overwhelming to a fourth grade teacher.

Fourth graders are great story writers but are often great tangent writers too. It is easy to write a story when you do not know where it is going. Getting fourth graders to stick to a structure is the challenge.

Three and four-paragraph essays are a good length for fourth graders. A structure which will train fourth graders for future expository writing is to write an opening paragraph which creates interest, two body paragraphs (one to compare, one to contrast), and a closing paragraph which links to the opening.

The closing paragraph is the most difficult for many students with the "I don't know what else to say" factor running very high. Students need to move away from closings like, "And that's the reason I told you about cats. I like them very much."

155

The habits students need to develop in fourth grade are that they simply cannot begin a paper without cleverly introducing the topic, and they cannot end a paper without making some reference to the opening paragraph (thus completing the "sandwich"). The body paragraphs deliver the information.

Fifth Grade

Thesis	Does not include a thesis statement.
Fmt	Uses words and phrases referring to the essay (This paragraph is ..., I'm going to talk about...).
Voc	Uses rich vocabulary but many of these words are misspelled.
Pgph	Each paragraph does not have a separate topic.
SS	Begins simple sentences with "and" or "but."
Fmt	Talks to the reader — "you will learn...," "you need to think about..."
SS	All sentences are of the same kind (simple).
Thesis	The thesis does not identify the purpose or topics of the body paragraphs.
Thesis	Too much information is given in the thesis — no need for the reader to read the remainder of the paper.
Pgph	Paragraphs are short and give few examples or none at all.

RW			
	a lot	before	does
	every	first	friend
	how	off	once
	right	said	talk
	then	to	until
	want	well	were
	when	where	who
	with		
	about	again	always
	are/our	because	didn't
	doesn't	English	know/now
	little	people	really

156

school	should	spelling
too	which	without
world	your	you're

Sp
already	all right	answer
beautiful	college	describe
different	enough	example
explain	favorite	language
question	remember	sentence
surprise	there/their	though
thought	wouldn't	

The fifth graders must focus on the thesis. Once they have learned that a thesis identifies specific topics, they next become practitioners at keeping each body paragraph on topic. Fifth grade is also where students must learn to describe with examples rather than repeating the same idea numerous times.

The opening and closing paragraphs will continue to be refined as they write them more and more, but the emphasis is on keeping body paragraphs on target with the thesis.

Paragraphs are still basic in their structure, but the five-paragraph essay can be a staple of the fifth grade (through ninth grade). The simple listing in the thesis of three topics is an easy structure to teach and for students to understand.

Much of what fifth graders practice is stepped up to the next level in sixth grade. If fifth graders can make it a habit of always including a thesis which identifies the topics of the body paragraphs, they have mastered a key component of effective writing.

Sixth Grade

Voc	Consecutive sentences end and then begin with the same word or phrase.
Voc	Body paragraphs begin with exact words as the thesis.
Fmt	The essay starts strong but each paragraph gets shorter.
Voc	All sentences begin the same way.
Voc	All paragraphs begin the same way.
Voc	Vocabulary — especially adjectives and verbs are too basic.
Punct	Dialogue is not indented or not punctuated correctly.
VT	Verb tense is inconsistent — past to present.
Pgph	Paragraphs end abruptly with no closing statement.
Voc	The same words or phrases are continually repeated in a paragraph.
VT	Writes narrative or story in present tense.
Ideas	Body paragraphs present examples but don't explain them.

RW

a lot	before	does
every	first	friend
how	off	once
right	said	talk
then	to	until
want	well	were
when	where	who
with		
about	again	always
are/our	because	didn't
doesn't	English	know/now
little	people	really
school	should	spelling
too	which	without
world	your	you're
already	all right	answer
beautiful	college	describe
different	enough	example

	explain	favorite	language
	question	remember	sentence
	surprise	there/their	though
	thought	wouldn't	
Sp	actually	another	corrected
	finally	knowledge	literature
	misspell	paragraph	science
	signed	sincerely	supposed to
	system	terrible	than
	tomorrow	trouble	vocabulary
	weather	whether	

The sixth grade writers should begin to stylize their writing to some degree. The goals in sixth grade are to refine the fifth grade skills and add substance and sophistication to their writing. Sixth graders today have heard and seen a lot. They are much more savvy than most of us would want them to be.

For most twelve to thirteen year old students, the sixth grade represents either the last year of elementary school or the first year of middle school or junior high. Needless to say, they are in transition. The more writing in which they can talk about themselves and their experiences, the more they will write.

My experience in sixth grade also indicates that as a group, they are not as willing to share their emotions by reading aloud in class. I find sixth graders to be much more guarded about exposing their feelings than are eighth graders. This may not be universal, but it is at least something to keep in mind as a teacher tries to prod students to dig deeper in their writing.

Seventh Grade

CP	Closing paragraph introduces new information.
Prs	The title does not generate interest or curiosity.
Ideas	Repeats the same idea in different words.
Voc	Vocabulary places too much emphasis on one syllable words.
SS	Writer is trying too hard to explain and sentences keeps circling around the same information.
Pgph	Topic of a paragraph is too broad or too narrow.
Pers	There is no emotion, personality, or warmth.
Voc	There is repetition of highly descriptive words in the same paragraph or essay.
Trans	Paragraphs introduce the next paragraph's topic in the closing sentence (early transition).

RW

a lot	before	does
every	first	friend
how	off	once
right	said	talk
then	to	until
want	well	were
when	where	who
with		
about	again	always
are/our	because	didn't
doesn't	English	know/now
little	people	really
school	should	spelling
too	which	without
world	your	you're
already	all right	answer
beautiful	college	describe
different	enough	example
explain	favorite	language
question	remember	sentence

160

surprise	there/their	though
thought	wouldn't	
actually	another	corrected
finally	knowledge	literature
misspell	paragraph	science
signed	sincerely	supposed to
system	terrible	than
tomorrow	trouble	vocabulary
weather	whether	

Sp	accurate	analyze	assignment
	believe	business	cooperation
	definite	difficult	difference
	emphasis	experiment	information
	interest	liquid	necessary
	obvious	occasion	receive
	recommend	separate	

By the time a student arrives in seventh grade, the span of writing abilities of individual students within a classroom can be daunting. There are students who can write remarkably well, and there are others who are still struggling with basics.

In a perfect world, students should have the structure of the essay (paragraphing, opening and closing paragraphs, and thesis) firmly within their grasp by the seventh grade. If they do not, then the teacher needs to treat these students as third, fourth, or fifth graders in teaching those skills. Forget the seventh grade skills. These students are not ready, and one cannot teach everything in one year.

For the average or high level seventh grader, refinement of vocabulary, clarity of wording, sophistication, and cleverness are key components. My constant prodding is,

161

"Be unique." One other element to consider with seventh graders is consistency. Their emotions are riding a roller coaster of highs and lows. They need a very structured, specific, and consistent approach to continue to improve on each paper.

Interesting topics are still essential, and since seventh graders seem to be at the apex of their self-centered world of adolescence, topics which are personal work the best.

Eighth Grade

CP	The closing paragraph has no twist — it ends abruptly or uses, "And that is why...."
Thesis	Each thesis item begins with the same word or phrase.
Usage	Uses nominative and objective case pronouns incorrectly.
Ideas	There are contradictory statements within a paragraph; says one thing, then says the opposite.
Voc	Overuse of verbs "am, is, are, was, were" and other non-descript verbs.
Punc	Overuse of the colon, hyphen, or quotations.
Thesis	Thesis items are not worded in the same tense or structure.
Ideas	Compares and contrasts in the same paragraph.
CP	Thesis is repeated in the same words in the closing.
CP	The link is similar or repeats the interest section of the opening paragraph.

RW			
	a lot	before	does
	every	first	friend
	how	off	once
	right	said	talk
	then	to	until
	want	well	were
	when	where	who
	with		
	about	again	always

are/our	because	didn't
doesn't	English	know/now
little	people	really
school	should	spelling
too	which	without
world	your	you're
already	all right	answer
beautiful	college	describe
different	enough	example
explain	favorite	language
question	remember	sentence
surprise	there/their	though
thought	wouldn't	
actually	another	corrected
finally	knowledge	literature
misspell	paragraph	science
signed	sincerely	supposed to
system	terrible	than
tomorrow	trouble	vocabulary
weather	whether	
accurate	analyze	assignment
believe	business	cooperation
definite	difficult	difference
emphasis	experiment	information
interest	liquid	necessary
obvious	occasion	receive
recommend	separate	

SP	accept/except	angle	argument
	belief	casual	committee
	continuous	decision	edible
	embarrass	exceed	naturally
	neutral	opportunity	past/passed
	proceed	relevant	succeed
	successful	weird	

In my experience, eighth graders are completely different from seventh graders. They have begun to make the transition into adulthood and exhibit much more sophistication in their writing. This is especially true during their second semester.

I also find that eighth graders are less obsessed with impressing their friends but are very concerned with pleasing themselves. This is not to say that eighth graders have moved past the trials and tribulations of junior high. It is just that they seem to have learned how to better deal with it, and they see a light at the end of the tunnel.

Given this level of maturity, eighth graders can do remarkable writing. In many cases, they can do some of the best writing of any grade level because they have had more experiences and yet are still relatively innocent. They have not quite accepted that certain things cannot happen so their writing can exhibit this unique point of view. In other words, the pressures of high school have not yet tainted them.

Ninth Grade

Use	There is disagreement in number (they, their, his, it, etc.).
Thesis	Thesis is too much of a pure listing of topics.
Ideas	Thoughts lack sophistication or "uniqueness."
Use	Overuse of contractions
CP	The link begins too abruptly. There is not a transition statement to begin the closing paragraph.
Thesis	Transition between interest and thesis is too abrupt or does not exist.
CP	The twist is not in keeping with the tone of the paper.
Pgph	The tone, style, or tense is not consistent between body paragraphs.
VT	Overuses the passive voice.
Prs	No personal style or indication of "who wrote this?"
Pgph	Three types of sentences do not appear in each paragraph.
Punc	One type of punctuation is overused.

RW

a lot	before	doe
every	first	friend
how	off	once
right	said	talk
then	to	until
want	well	were
when	where	who
with		
about	again	always
are/our	because	didn't
doesn't	English	know/now
little	people	really
school	should	spelling
too	which	without
world	your	you're
already	all right	answer
beautiful	college	describe
different	enough	example
explain	favorite	language
question	remember	sentence
surprise	there/their	though
thought	wouldn't	
actually	another	corrected
finally	knowledge	literature
misspell	paragraph	science
signed	sincerely	supposed to
system	terrible	than
tomorrow	trouble	vocabulary
weather	whether	
accurate	analyze	assignment
believe	business	cooperation
definite	difficult	difference
emphasis	experiment	information
interest	liquid	necessary
obvious	occasion	receive
recommend	separate	
accept/except	angle	argument
belief	casual	committee
continuous	decision	edible
embarrass	exceed	naturally
neutral	opportunity	past/passed
proceed	relevant	succeed
successful	weird	

Ninth grade students are typically beginning the distinct stratification into college-bound versus general education students. The teacher is also usually tied to a more traditional set of novels, plays, and short stories which often become the focus of the writing program. This is not to say that this does not occur in seventh and eighth grades, but it seems to definitely rise to the forefront in ninth grade.

The college-bound students still exhibit a wide range in their writing ability, but since many less-qualified students have extracted themselves from this echelon, the range is more workable.

The teachers who work with the general education students must continue to apply the hierarchy of skills previously described. There are many ninth graders who fall within the writing ability of third through eighth graders. All the teacher can do is place them in the appropriate grade level hierarchy and establish the year-end goal paper.

If a ninth grade student has not learned paragraphing and sentence structure in ten years of schooling, there are four possible reasons: He or she has had poor instruction, the student has never tried, the student is a transitional language student, or the student simply does not have the ability to learn the material.

If poor instruction or lack of expectation by past teachers is the culprit, you can make a difference. If the student does not care, then he or she will either continue to ask to be failed or will undergo an attitude change. Your chances of reaching this student are 50/50. If the student is in language transition, a grade level hierarchy is exactly what he or she needs. If the student lacks the ability, press the issue with special education.

Of all the skills a student learns in school, those which he or she must master are reading and writing. Life will never be as pleasant for a student who cannot read and cannot write.

The grade level task analysis listed above is teacher-centered; the following lists are for the student. These are the skills which a student must apply at each grade level to stay on target.

Within each school in every school district this list must be revised and adapted. These examples are listed as a model only; however, imagine the integration of information if every third through ninth grade student were supplied with this type of consistent approach. Writing can be reduced to a measurable outcome.

Much of the information in the following pages is redundant. It is presented again so teachers may copy or scan these pages for classroom use.

THIRD GRADE WRITING GUIDE

ESSENTIAL FOR NEXT YEAR

a lot	before	does
every	first	friend
how	off	once
right	said	talk
then	to	until
want	well	were
when	where	who
with		

COMMA RULES

Rule 1: Use a comma to offset an introductory word.
Rule 2:
Rule 3: Use a comma between three or more items in a series.
Rule 4:
Rule 5:
Rule 6 Use a comma between days, dates, and years.
Rule 7: Use a comma in the salutation in a friendly letter.
Rule 8: Use a comma between cities and states but NOT between states and zip codes
Rule 9:
Rule 10:

CAPITALIZATION RULES

Rule 1:
Rule 2:
Rule 3:
Rule 4:
Rule 5: Capitalize all words in a title.

Rule -1:

Rule -2: Do not capitalize summer, winter, spring, fall, sun, moon, star, planet.

Rule -3:

Rule -4:

Rule -5:

WRITING ASSIGNMENT CHECKLIST

Is your heading complete?

Is your title capitalized properly?

Is there a capital letter after each period?

Is each paragraph indented?

Is there more than one paragraph?

Are there any sentences that are only three words in length?

Are there any sentences that are longer than fifteen words?

Are there at least two sentences in each paragraph?

Did you write on every line — not skipping any?

Did you read your paper aloud or have someone read your paper aloud to you?

FOURTH GRADE WRITING GUIDE

REWRITE WORDS

a lot	before	does
every	first	friend
how	off	once
right	said	talk
then	to	until
want	well	were
when	where	who
with		

ESSENTIAL FOR NEXT YEAR

about	again	always
are/our	because	didn't
doesn't	English	know
little	now	people
really	school	should
spelling	which	without
world	your	you're

COMMA RULES

Rule 1:   Use a comma to offset an introductory word.

Rule 2:   Use a comma between two descriptive adjectives which can be reversed in order.

Rule 3:   Use a comma between three or more items in a series.

Rule 4:

Rule 5:

Rule 6:   Use a comma between days, dates, and years.

Rule 7:   Use a comma in the salutation in a friendly letter.

Rule 8:   Use a comma between cities and states but NOT between states and zip codes.

Rule 9:

Rule 10:

CAPITALIZATION RULES

Rule 1: Capitalize any word that would appear on a map.

Rule 2: Capitalize any word that would appear on a store-bought calendar.

Rule 3: Capitalize any word which would appear on a person's name tag at a meeting or family reunion.

Rule 4: Capitalize any word which would appear on the sign in front of a building.

Rule 5: Capitalize all words in a title.

Rule -1:

Rule -2: Do not capitalize summer, winter, spring, fall, sun, moon, star, planet.

Rule -3: Do not capitalize names of family relations when they are preceded by a possessive pronoun.

Rule -4: Do not capitalize north, south, east, west or any combinations when they say which way you are going. (Usually, these are capitalized after the word "the.")

Rule -5:

WRITING ASSIGNMENT CHECKLIST

Is your heading complete?

Is your title capitalized properly?

Is there a capital letter after each period?

Did you correct all of the instant rewrite words?

Is each paragraph indented?

Is there more than one paragraph — three or more?

Are there any sentences that are only three words in length?

Are there any sentences that are longer than fifteen words?

Are there at least three sentences in each paragraph?

Did you write on every line — not skipping any?

Is your assignment in cursive or typed?

Did you apply all of the comma rules?

Did you apply all of the capitalization rules?

Did you read your paper aloud or have someone read your paper aloud to you?

FIFTH GRADE WRITING GUIDE

REWRITE WORDS

a lot	before	does
every	first	friend
how	off	once
right	said	talk
then	to	until
want	well	were
when	where	who
with		
about	again	always
are/our	because	didn't
doesn't	English	know
little	now	people
really	school	should
spelling	which	without
world	your	you're

ESSENTIAL FOR NEXT YEAR

already	all right	answer
beautiful	college	describe
different	enough	example
explain	favorite	language
question	remember	sentence
surprise	there/their	though
thought	wouldn't	

COMMA RULES

Rule 1: Use a comma to offset an introductory word or phrase.
Rule 2: Use a comma between two descriptive adjectives which can be reversed in order.
Rule 3: Use a comma between three or more items in a series.
Rule 4: Use a comma before "and, but, or, nor, for, yet" when there is a complete sentence on either side.
Rule 5:
Rule 6 Use a comma between days, dates, and years.
Rule 7: Use a comma in the salutation in a friendly letter.
Rule 8: Use a comma between cities and states but NOT between states and zip codes.
Rule 9: Use a comma to offset quotes unless you use a ? or !
Rule 10:

CAPITALIZATION RULES

Rule 1: Capitalize any word that would appear on a map.
Rule 2: Capitalize any word that would appear on a store-bought calendar.
Rule 3: Capitalize any word which would appear on a person's name tag at a meeting or family reunion.
Rule 4: Capitalize any word which would appear on the sign in front of a building.
Rule 5: Capitalize all words in a title except for articles, conjunctions, and prepositions.

Rule -1: Do not capitalize a school subject unless it is a language or numbered course (History 101).
Rule -2: Do not capitalize summer, winter, spring, fall, sun, moon, star, planet.
Rule -3: Do not capitalize names of family relations when they are preceded by a possessive pronoun.
Rule -4: Do not capitalize north, south, east, west or any combinations when they say which way you are going. (Usually, these are capitalized after the word "the.")
Rule -5: Do not capitalize the word after a hyphen unless it follows a capitalization rule.

WRITING ASSIGNMENT CHECKLIST

Is your heading complete?
Is your title capitalized properly?
Is there a capital letter after each period?
Did you correct all of the instant rewrite words?
Is each paragraph indented?
Are there at least three paragraphs?
Is there a clear thesis statement in your opening paragraph?
Is there an opening paragraph?
Is there at least one body paragraph?
Is there a closing paragraph?
Are there any sentences that are only three words in length?
Are there any sentences that are longer than fifteen words?
Are there at least three sentences in each paragraph?
Did you write on every line — not skipping any?
Do you repeat any descriptive word more than twice in any paragraph or sentence?
Is your assignment in cursive or typed?
Did you apply all of the comma rules?
Did you apply all of the capitalization rules?

Did you read your paper aloud or have someone read your paper
    aloud to you?
Does each paragraph begin with a topic sentence?

SIXTH GRADE WRITING GUIDE

REWRITE WORDS

a lot	before	does
every	first	friend
how	off	once
right	said	talk
then	to	until
want	well	were
when	where	who
with		
about	again	always
are/our	because	didn't
doesn't	English	know
little	now	people
really	school	should
spelling	which	without
world	your	you're
already	all right	answer
beautiful	college	describe
different	enough	example
explain	favorite	language
question	remember	sentence
surprise	there/their	though
thought	wouldn't	

ESSENTIAL FOR NEXT YEAR

actually	another	corrected
finally	knowledge	literature
misspell	paragraph	science
signed	sincerely	supposed
system	terrible	than
tomorrow	trouble	vocabulary
weather	whether	

COMMA RULES

Rule 1:   Use a comma to offset an introductory word or phrase.
Rule 2:   Use a comma between two descriptive adjectives which can be reversed in order.
Rule 3:   Use a comma between three or more items in a series.
Rule 4:   Use a comma before "and, but, or, nor, for, yet" when there is a complete sentence on either side.
Rule 5:   Use a comma to offset appositives and words in direct address.
Rule 6   Use a comma between days, dates, and years.
Rule 7:   Use a comma in the salutation in a friendly letter.
Rule 8:   Use a comma between cities and states but NOT between states and zip codes.
Rule 9:   Use a comma to offset quotes unless you use a ? or !
Rule 10:

CAPITALIZATION RULES

Rule 1:   Capitalize any word that would appear on a map.
Rule 2:   Capitalize any word that would appear on a store-bought calendar.
Rule 3:   Capitalize any word which would appear on a person's name tag at a meeting or family reunion.
Rule 4:   Capitalize any word which would appear on the sign in front of a building.
Rule 5:   Capitalize all words in a title except for articles, conjunctions, and prepositions.

Rule -1: Do not capitalize a school subject unless it is a language or numbered course (History 101).
Rule -2: Do not capitalize summer, winter, spring, fall, sun, moon, star, planet.
Rule -3: Do not capitalize names of family relations when they are preceded by a possessive pronoun.
Rule -4: Do not capitalize north, south, east, west or any combinations when they say which way you are going. (Usually, these are capitalized after the word "the.")
Rule -5: Do not capitalize the word after a hyphen unless it follows a capitalization rule.

WRITING ASSIGNMENT CHECKLIST

Is your heading complete?
Is your title capitalized properly?
Is there a capital letter after each period?
Did you correct all of the instant rewrite words?
Is each paragraph indented?
Are there at least four paragraphs?
Is there a clear thesis statement in your opening paragraph?
Are there at least two body paragraphs?
Is there a closing paragraph?
Are there any sentences that are only four words in length?
Are there any sentences that are longer than fifteen words?
Are there at least four sentences in each paragraph?
Did you write on every line — not skipping any?
Is your assignment in cursive or typed?
Did you write the dialogue properly?
Did you apply all of the comma rules?
Are all paragraphs of similar length?
Did you apply all of the capitalization rules?
Did you read your paper aloud or have someone read your paper aloud to you?
Does each paragraph begin with a topic sentence?
Does each paragraph end with a closing statement that makes the reader feel it is complete?
Do any two sentences in the same paragraph begin the same way?
Do any two consecutive sentences end and begin the same way?
Did you use any strong words more than once (twice) in the same paragraph?
Did you tell the story in the past tense?

SEVENTH GRADE WRITING GUIDE

REWRITE WORDS

a lot
every
how
right
then
want
when
with
about
are/our
doesn't
little
really
spelling
world
already
beautiful
different
explain
question
surprise
thought
actually
finally
misspell
signed
system
tomorrow
weather

before
first
off
said
to
well
where

again
because
English
now
school
which
your
all right
college
enough
favorite
remember
there/their
wouldn't
another
knowledge
paragraph
sincerely
terrible
trouble
whether

does
friend
once
talk
until
were
who

always
didn't
know
people
should
without
you're
answer
describe
example
language
sentence
though

corrected
literature
science
supposed
than
vocabulary

ESSENTIAL FOR NEXT YEAR

accurate
believe
definite
emphasis
interest
obvious
recommend

analyze
business
difficult
experiment
liquid
occasion
separate

assignment
cooperation
difference
information
necessary
receive

COMMA RULES

Rule 1: Use a comma to offset an introductory word or phrase.

Rule 2: Use a comma between two descriptive adjectives which can be reversed in order.

Rule 3: Use a comma between three or more items in a series.

Rule 4: Use a comma before "and, but, or, nor, for, yet" when there is a complete sentence on either side.

Rule 5: Use a comma to offset appositives and words in direct address.

Rule 6 Use a comma between days, dates, and years.

Rule 7: Use a comma in the salutation in a friendly letter.

Rule 8: Use a comma between cities and states but NOT between states and zip codes.

Rule 9: Use a comma to offset quotes unless you use a ? or !

Rule 10: Use a comma where a natural pause is necessary or to avoid confusing wordings.

CAPITALIZATION RULES

Rule 1: Capitalize any word that would appear on a map.

Rule 2: Capitalize any word that would appear on a store-bought calendar.

Rule 3: Capitalize any word which would appear on a person's name tag at a meeting or family reunion.

Rule 4: Capitalize any word which would appear on the sign in front of a building.

Rule 5: Capitalize all words in a title except for articles, conjunctions, and prepositions.

Rule -1: Do not capitalize a school subject unless it is a language or numbered course (History 101).

Rule -2: Do not capitalize summer, winter, spring, fall, sun, moon, star, planet.

Rule -3: Do not capitalize names of family relations when they are preceded by a possessive pronoun.

Rule -4: Do not capitalize north, south, east, west or any combinations when they say which way you are going. (Usually, these are capitalized after the word "the.")

Rule -5: Do not capitalize the word after a hyphen unless it follows a capitalization rule.

WRITING ASSIGNMENT CHECKLIST

Is your heading complete?

Is your title capitalized properly?

Is there a capital letter after each period?

Did you correct all of the instant rewrite words?

Is each paragraph indented?

Are there at least four paragraphs?

Is there a clear thesis statement in your opening paragraph?

Are there at least two body paragraphs?

Is there a closing paragraph?

Are there any sentences that are fewer than five words in length?

Are there any sentences that are longer than fifteen words?

Are there at least five sentences in each paragraph?

Did you write on every line — not skipping any?

Is your assignment in cursive or typed?

Do you repeat any descriptive word more than twice in any paragraph or sentence?

Did you write the dialogue properly?

Did you apply all of the comma rules?

Are all paragraphs of similar length?

Did you apply all of the capitalization rules?

Did you read your paper aloud or have someone read your paper aloud to you?

Does each paragraph begin with a topic sentence?

Does each paragraph end with a closing statement that makes the reader feel it is complete?

Is there a transition word beginning at least one of your body paragraphs?

Does your transition always begin a paragraph?

Do any two sentences in the same paragraph begin the same way?

Do any two consecutive sentences end and begin the same way?

Do any two paragraphs begin the same way?

Did you use any strong words more than once in the same paragraph?

Did you tell the story in the past tense?

EIGHTH GRADE WRITING GUIDE

REWRITE WORDS

a lot	before	does
every	first	friend
how	off	once
right	said	talk
then	to	until
want	well	were
when	where	who
with		
about	again	always
are/our	because	didn't
doesn't	English	know
little	now	people
really	school	should
spelling	which	without
world	your	you're
already	all right	answer
beautiful	college	describe
different	enough	example
explain	favorite	language
question	remember	sentence
surprise	there/their	though
thought	wouldn't	
actually	another	corrected
finally	knowledge	literature
misspell	paragraph	science
signed	sincerely	supposed
system	terrible	than
tomorrow	trouble	vocabulary
weather	whether	
accurate	analyze	assignment
believe	business	cooperation
definite	difficult	difference
emphasis	experiment	information
interest	liquid	necessary
obvious	occasion	receive
recommend	separate	

ESSENTIAL FOR NEXT YEAR

accept/except	angle	argument
belief	casual	committee
continuous	decision	edible
embarrass	exceed	naturally
neutral	opportunity	past/passed
proceed	relevant	succeed
successful	weird	

COMMA RULES

Rule 1: Use a comma to offset an introductory word or phrase.
Rule 2: Use a comma between two descriptive adjectives which can be reversed in order.
Rule 3: Use a comma between three or more items in a series.
Rule 4: Use a comma before "and, but, or, nor, for, yet" when there is a complete sentence on either side.
Rule 5: Use a comma to offset appositives and words in direct address.
Rule 6 Use a comma between days, dates, and years.
Rule 7: Use a comma in the salutation in a friendly letter.
Rule 8: Use a comma between cities and states but NOT between states and zip codes.
Rule 9: Use a comma to offset quotes unless you use a ? or !
Rule 10: Use a comma where a natural pause is necessary or to avoid confusing wordings.

CAPITALIZATION RULES

Rule 1: Capitalize any word that would appear on a map.
Rule 2: Capitalize any word that would appear on a store-bought calendar.
Rule 3: Capitalize any word which would appear on a person's name tag at a meeting or family reunion.
Rule 4: Capitalize any word which would appear on the sign in front of a building.
Rule 5: Capitalize all words in a title except for articles, conjunctions, and prepositions.

Rule -1: Do not capitalize a school subject unless it is a language or numbered course (History 101).
Rule -2: Do not capitalize summer, winter, spring, fall, sun, moon, star, planet.
Rule -3: Do not capitalize names of family relations when they are preceded by a possessive pronoun.
Rule -4: Do not capitalize north, south, east, west or any combinations when they say which way you are going. (Usually, these are capitalized after the word "the.")
Rule -5: Do not capitalize the word after a hyphen unless it follows a capitalization rule.

WRITING ASSIGNMENT CHECKLIST

Is your heading complete?

Is your title capitalized properly?

Is there a capital letter after each period?

Did you correct all of the instant rewrite words?

Is each paragraph indented?

Are there at least four paragraphs?

Is there a clear thesis statement and does each thesis item worded in the same tense or structure?

Are there at least two body paragraphs?

Does your closing paragraph restate the thesis in different words?

Are there any sentences that are fewer than five words in length?

Are there any sentences that are longer than twenty words?

Are there at least five sentences in each paragraph?

Did you write on every line — not skipping any?

Is your assignment in cursive or typed?

Do you repeat any descriptive word more than twice in any paragraph or sentence?

Did you write the dialogue properly?

Did you apply all of the comma rules?

Are all paragraphs of similar length?

Did you apply all of the capitalization rules?

Did you read your paper aloud or have someone read your paper aloud to you?

Does each paragraph begin with a topic sentence that differs from the wording of the thesis?

Does each paragraph end with a closing statement that makes the reader feel it is complete?

Is there a transition word beginning at least one of your body paragraphs?

Does your transition always begin a paragraph?

Do any two sentences in the same paragraph begin the same way?

Do any two consecutive sentences end and begin the same way?

Do any two paragraphs begin the same way?

Did you use any strong words more than once within a paragraph?

Did you tell the story in the past tense?

NINTH GRADE WRITING GUIDE

REWRITE WORDS

a lot	before	does
every	first	friend
how	off	once
right	said	talk
then	to	until
want	well	were
when	where	who
with		
about	again	always
are/our	because	didn't
doesn't	English	know
little	now	people
really	school	should
spelling	which	without
world	your	you're
already	all right	answer
beautiful	college	describe
different	enough	example
explain	favorite	language
question	remember	sentence
surprise	there/their	though
thought	wouldn't	
actually	another	corrected
finally	knowledge	literature
misspell	paragraph	science
signed	sincerely	supposed
system	terrible	than
tomorrow	trouble	vocabulary
weather	whether	
accurate	analyze	assignment
believe	business	cooperation
definite	difficult	difference
emphasis	experiment	information
interest	liquid	necessary
obvious	occasion	receive
recommend	separate	
accept/except	angle	argument
belief	casual	committee
continuous	decision	edible
embarrass	exceed	naturally
neutral	opportunity	past/passed
proceed	relevant	succeed
successful	weird	

COMMA RULES

Rule 1: Use a comma to offset an introductory word or phrase.
Rule 2: Use a comma between two descriptive adjectives which can be reversed in order.
Rule 3: Use a comma between three or more items in a series.
Rule 4: Use a comma before "and, but, or, nor, for, yet" when there is a complete sentence on either side.
Rule 5: Use a comma to offset appositives and words in direct address.
Rule 6 Use a comma between days, dates, and years.
Rule 7: Use a comma in the salutation in a friendly letter.
Rule 8: Use a comma between cities and states but NOT between states and zip codes.
Rule 9: Use a comma to offset quotes unless you use a ? or !
Rule 10: Use a comma where a natural pause is necessary or to avoid confusing wordings.

CAPITALIZATION RULES

Rule 1: Capitalize any word that would appear on a map.
Rule 2: Capitalize any word that would appear on a store-bought calendar.
Rule 3: Capitalize any word which would appear on a person's name tag at a meeting or family reunion.
Rule 4: Capitalize any word which would appear on the sign in front of a building.
Rule 5: Capitalize all words in a title except for articles, conjunctions, and prepositions.

Rule -1: Do not capitalize a school subject unless it is a language or numbered course (History 101).
Rule -2: Do not capitalize summer, winter, spring, fall, sun, moon, star, planet.
Rule -3: Do not capitalize names of family relations when they are preceded by a possessive pronoun.
Rule -4: Do not capitalize north, south, east, west or any combinations when they say which way you are going. (Usually, these are capitalized after the word "the.")
Rule -5: Do not capitalize the word after a hyphen unless it follows a capitalization rule.

WRITING ASSIGNMENT CHECKLIST

Is your heading complete?

Is your title capitalized properly?

Is there a capital letter after each period?

Did you correct all of the instant rewrite words?

Are there at least four paragraphs, and is each paragraph indented?

Is there a clear thesis statement and is each thesis item worded in the same tense or structure?

Is there an opening paragraph?

Does your closing paragraph restate the thesis in different words, and does it avoid simply listing the topics?

Are there any sentences that are fewer than five words in length?

Are there any sentences that are longer than twenty words?

Are there at least five sentences in each paragraph, and are there different types of sentences within each paragraph?

Did you write on every line — not skipping any?

Is your assignment in cursive or typed?

Do you repeat any descriptive word more than twice in any paragraph or sentence?

Did you write the dialogue properly?

Did you apply all of the comma and capitalization rules?

Do all paragraphs contain a similar tone, tense, and style?

Did you read your paper aloud or have someone read your paper aloud to you?

Does each paragraph begin with a topic sentence that differs from the wording of the thesis?

Does each paragraph end with a closing statement that makes the reader feel it is complete?

Is there a transition word beginning at least one of your body paragraphs?

Does your transition always begin a paragraph?

Do any two sentences in the same paragraph begin the same way?

Do any two consecutive sentences end and begin the same way?

Do any two paragraphs begin the same way?

Did you use any strong words more than once within a paragraph?

Did you tell the story in the past tense?

The most glaring omission in this task analysis is the minimal reference to the creativity and personality of writing. The levels of creativity and students' ability to put themselves into their writing have no specific grade level boundaries. I have read papers by third graders in which I could almost hear the student smiling through words. In contrast, I have read papers from eighth graders that seem more robotic than human.

To try and incorporate these ingredients in this hierarchy would be pointless. At every grade level, within the confines or structure of writing, the teacher is the one who brings the student out of himself or herself. The creativity of the assignment is the determining element in the amount of personality you will see in your students' writing.

In the chapter, "Superficial versus Personal writing," an explanation of types of assignments and their affect on motivation is presented in depth. To paraphrase that entire chapter in one sentence: The more life experience the student can bring to an assignment, the more creativity he or she will demonstrate in the writing.

The hierarchy of student writing which is presented here will continue to undergo a metamorphosis. It has already been emphasized that this is merely a sample. Take what you can use and apply it to your situation. I have tried to provide a model that removes some of the mystery for my students. The secret is to adapt my program to help remove the mystique for the students with whom you are working.

Sample Assignments

In an earlier chapter, I described my philosophy regarding students doing sixteen writing assignments per year and distributing these assignments in sets of two. To briefly reiterate my reasoning: It is much less time-consuming to plan eight sets of related writing assignments than to plan sixteen different tasks. When students have two similar assignments, they can apply what they have learned in writing the first to the second.

This approach is not intended to replace the typical teaching that occurs in science, social studies, and literature. Rather, linking all writing to content areas is meant to enrich and expand the students' understanding while at the same time saving the teacher the responsibility (and time) of providing a different, non-connected writing curriculum. The writing becomes the application of the learning.

In this chapter I present twenty sets of assignments. In compiling this information, I had to decide whether or not to make them grade level specific, simplify all of them allowing upper grade teachers to add information, or enhance all of them requiring lower grade teachers to simplify. My decision was to do the latter. It always seems easier to look at the complete picture and then extract the parts that are appropriate or which I can use.

Me, Myself, and I: Autobiography

The autobiography is a nice place to start each year since it allows the teacher to learn about the individual student. I have always thought that an outstanding project would be to have students begin their personal autobiography in the third grade and add new information each year. By the time a student graduates from high school, it would be a synopsis of their childhood experiences and emotions. The coordination of this would be impossible, but it would be a remarkable document.

Clearly, these two assignments are not related to content areas for self-contained teachers. During the first several weeks of the school year, teachers typically filter content areas into the curriculum rather slowly. There is diagnostic testing, the initial period of getting to know students, and often the introductory chapters of a science and social studies book lack true content. These assignments will get students writing from the first day; therefore, I am suggesting that they write simply for the sake of writing. I find autobiographies provide interesting insight at the beginning of a school year.

Essay 1:

Over these two weeks you will be writing an autobiographical essay. Your paper will be four paragraphs long and will contain an opening and closing paragraph and two body paragraphs.

Your opening paragraph should create interest by using a personal anecdote describing something that happened to you in the past. This event must be different than any of the events you describe in the body paragraphs. You will then need a thesis sentence which introduces your two body paragraph topics.

Your closing paragraph must link to the anecdote you described in the opening, it must restate your thesis in different terms, and then must have a twist at the very end which makes me smile or nod as I read it.

You may choose from the following topics for body paragraphs:

1. Your very first recollection as a child.
2. A time you were most embarrassed.
3. A time you were most proud.
4. A pet that meant a lot to you.
5. A first vacation that you vividly remember.
6. A toy or gift that was extremely meaningful.
7. A time you were most sad, hurt, or confused.
8. The funniest thing that ever happened to you — a time you could not stop laughing.
9. Clear any other topics with me but feel free to create your own.

Essay 2:

This is an extension of the first essay in that you will now add a prologue and epilogue to your autobiography and add four more body paragraphs. The body paragraphs must use topics suggested in 1-9 above (you have only written about two of them thus far); however, the ninth choice gives you the freedom to select other topics of interest.

The prologue is a two or three sentence statement that establishes your birth date, and the epilogue is two or three more sentences at the close of your paper which briefly describe your outlook for the future.

Sample Prologue

Two inches of snow fell in downtown Los Angeles. Children and adults alike ran outside to hurl snowballs at one another. It was indeed a memorable day. Christmas had come and gone four days before, and 1979 would soon be ushered in. Somewhere in the midst of the holiday and snow, I was born — December 29, 1978.

By the time this essay is due, you will have received your corrected copy of essay 1. You must make suggested corrections on the first essay and insert the topics of essay 2 into the original thesis statement. You must also add your prologue on a separate sheet of paper (as if it were a title page) and the epilogue on a separate sheet of paper (as if it were an afterthought). When you hand in the complete version on your autobiography, it will contain the following:

Prologue (separate page) + opening paragraph + six body paragraphs + closing paragraph + epilogue (separate page)

Vocabulary for this unit:

scapegoat	personal	relative
sibling	decisive	trauma
pariah	negligent	diversion
obnoxious	detour	jealous
overshadowed	enigma	detached
boisterous	transpire	declare
internal	external	influence

bite the bullet
chip on your shoulder

Inventions and How Things Work

My students have particularly enjoyed the second essay of this set. If you are teaching a self-contained class, one (or several) of the chapters in the science book will describe how natural phenomenon occur. There are many writing opportunities in the areas of life and earth science, but this inventions essay works particularly well with physical science, especially the units focusing on energy, physics, or simple machines.

Another possible content curriculum match is the Industrial Revolution, the Greeks, or the Renaissance in social studies. In my classroom, I would wait until I began teaching the historical unit on a time of enlightenment and teach the science unit on simple machines at the same time. The two essays will fit perfectly with this combination, and the vocabulary has a strong overlap.

Essay 1:

Pick a natural phenomenon or an invention and write a 400 to 600 word explanation of how or why it works or occurs. We will create a list of twenty or so possible topics in class. Some sample topics are: Why is the sky blue? Why does a guitar sound different than a piano? What are thunder and lightning? Why is there sand on the beach? How do fiber optic cables work? Why is it colder in the mountains if they are closer to the sun?

Your essay must be written in first person, using "I," and must be in your words. I am not looking for a technical description. You must explain your topic in words that will be clear to your classmates. You will have to describe your subject to the class without the use of your paper, so you need to truly understand it!

Begin your paper with a minimum three-sentence personal experience which connects you to the topic and provide a clear, one-sentence thesis statement. Your paper should be a minimum of three paragraphs (opening, body, and closing). Your closing must restate your thesis, refer to your personal connection to the topic, and must include a twist.

Essay 2:

Use your imagination to create an invention. Your essay should be 500 to 800 words in length and contain at least five paragraphs (opening, three body paragraphs, and closing). Explain how your invention works, why it is important, who will use it, what it is made of, etc. Your opening paragraph should create interest by asking three or more questions to gain the reader's interest and must have a clear thesis which identifies the purpose of each body paragraph. We will discuss this thoroughly in class.

You will also need to either draw a picture or create a three dimensional model of your invention to share with your classmates. My suggestion is you keep your creation a secret so your classmates don't "borrow" your idea.

Vocabulary for this unit:

prototype	mock-up	Beta test
CAD	patent	blueprint
mechanism	Imagineering	trend
scale model	schematic	insomnia
predecessor	cutting edge	synthetic
natural selection	R & D	refinement
alteration	influx	technology
rehabilitate	catnap	dynamic

Thomas Edison   Johan Gutenberg   Henry Ford
Bill Gates

Necessity is the mother of invention
Back to the drawing board

History of the World — the Top 100

The first essay in this set is a basic report of information and would fit well with a science or social studies unit which presents a number of proper names. Possible content topics might include: explorers (Columbus, Coronado, etc.), Greek or Egyptian history, the Civil War, the Constitutional Congress, astronomy/space, mathematicians in geometry, or influential community members (third grade).

Essay 2 might be written about the same person as in the first essay or could be assigned as a book report on a biography the students are reading for language arts.

Essay 1:

Choose a person from one of the books in class, or select a person who you think should be considered to be one of the 100 most important people in the history of the world. You may not choose a sports figure, musical performer, or movie star who has been popular since 1950. You may choose others who are more current — world leaders, architects, writers, etc.

You must identify at least two, but not more than three, reasons why this person is/was so important. These will be your body paragraphs. Your opening paragraph should create interest by putting the person in his or her historical context — when, where, why, etc. This should be three to four sentences followed by a thesis which presents two or three accomplishments.

I do not want to see the life story of this person. I want you to explain why he or she was so influential.

Your closing paragraph must link, restate and twist (as always), and your essay should be 500 to 600 words in length.

Essay 2:

Using the person you wrote about in your first essay, you must pretend that you are a friend or acquaintance and you must either: Do an interview, talk show style, with your person, or write an essay explaining what it is like to be his or her friend. With either approach, describe personality and your relationship with the person.

Your opening should begin with a personal anecdote or story involving you and this person. Remember that if he or she was alive in 1700, you must write as though it is the 1700's now. None of the inventions, comforts, or history since that time would exist. Your thesis should identify two or three recollections, impressions, or impacts during your friendship with your famous person.

Vocabulary for this unit:

philosopher	spiritual	secular
monarchy	Hindu	Buddhist
Moslem	Christian	orator
benevolent	fictitious	theory
emperor	anarchist	enigma
mythical	imperialist	outcast
breakthrough	heretic	nirvana
euphoria	egocentric	invaluable

Father Time	Grim Reaper	Big Brother
Mother Nature		

The bigger they are, the harder they fall.
It's not what you know, it's who you know.

Back to the Future . . .

The concept of the time machine is magical to most students, and every time I give these assignments I get remarkable writing. In terms of a link with content, these essays connect to any unit in history, prehistoric times to the nineteen-sixties. In science, connections can be made to units on fossils, paleontology, archeology, simple machines, or atomic energy.

A coordinating book report genre might be science fiction or a non-fiction book on architecture or a specific period in history.

Essay 1:

This is a five paragraph essay in which you must use your imagination to create a day in the future or past. You can project ten years, fifty years, a hundred years, or more. You are still you (as you are today), but you have arrived in this future or past time through use of a time machine. You must select three aspects of this world to describe in your body paragraphs.

Your opening paragraph must create interest in a minimum of four sentences, imagining that you have just now arrived in this setting — explain how you are feeling and what you see. You must also include a thesis in the opening paragraph which introduces the three features of the world that you are going to discuss.

Minimum length is 500 words. It must also have five paragraphs — opening, three body, and closing paragraphs.

Essay 2:

In this essay, you must return to the same time period as your first essay. Imagine that you are ninety years old and are describing your life to your grandchildren. You have more freedom as to the structure of this essay, but you must include an opening paragraph which creates interest by using a quote or a song lyric. You must explain why this quote is symbolic of the ninety years that you have been alive.

Your closing paragraph must also link to this quote or lyric. Minimum length is 450 words.

Vocabulary for this unit:

warp	millennium	century
utopia	flashback	premonition
conventional	modification	negligible
oasis	aura	idealistic
inundate	mutation	degrade
infiltrate	surreal	decompose
transpire	habitat	visionary
architecture	Armageddon	ancestor

George Orwell   Nostradamus   Orson Wells

Does anyone really know what time it is?
Timing is everything

Making Sense of It All: Descriptive Essay

If assigned exactly as described below, these two essays would typically be categorized as "descriptive;" however, they will work very well in any type of application in which an "observational" approach is required. Content area links might include science experiments (especially slowly changing events such as the metamorphosis from caterpillar to butterfly, the budding of a flower or leaf, or decaying of fruit), the night sky (meteor showers, eclipse, or constellations), environmental studies, or meteorology.

In social studies, either essay might be used within a unit in which one specific event or location changed the course of human events. Examples like the atomic bomb, D-day, Gettysburg, or the eruption of Mount Vesuvius would be appropriate. The fundamental purpose of both essays is to create an emotional or sensory response through the use of vivid language.

Essay 1:

For both the first and second essay in this unit, you will write about a picture which you must select. It can be a photograph or a picture from a magazine. You are going to use the same picture for both essays so make certain it is something that is interesting to you.

It is best if you choose a photograph of an outdoor scene. There can be people but no more than three.

In the first essay you must describe the picture so I can vividly visualize it in my mind without seeing it! After I have read your paper, I will look at the picture, and one third of your grade will be based on how well you created the image in my mind. Please note the following when writing

1. You need to be very specific about describing precise colors (use similes: "like a. . .").

2. You must tell me the location of the various items in the picture — what is in front, in the back, etc. (one body paragraph).

3. You must tell me what the mood or tone of the picture is (the weather, perhaps in a second body paragraph).

4. You may not use the words "picture" or "photograph" at any time in your essay. You must imagine that you are physically there.

5. Remember that you have five senses; I want you to use words that appeal to all five senses when you describe the scene.

6. Be very careful not to overuse the words: am, is, are, was, or were.

7. Create interest by describing how essential your senses are to your existence, and close your essay with a similar reminder of the importance of your senses.

Essay 2:

You must become one of the objects (not a person) in your picture and write a five or six paragraph essay describing your impression of the seasons that you experience. This will be written in first person (I). You must imagine what it is like to be that thing surviving or existing in nature.

Vocabulary for this unit:

image	solitude	translucent
transparent	opaque	balmy

indifferent	ornate	ascending
descending	primitive	knoll
dismal	expanse	intricate
abyss	chasm	fortress
sentinel	vast	excessive

Ansel Adams   Henry David Thoreau   John Muir
Walden

Beauty is in the eyes of the beholder.
After nature, only the copyist.

The Best of Times and the Worst of Times

These assignments are very simple. The challenge is for students to make the second essay sound different than the first. An opportunity in teaching these assignments is to discuss "tone." To look for a specific and different tone whether it be sarcasm, irony, optimism, etc., is the goal.

For departmentalized teachers, linking these to a content area is a bit more of a challenge. The link I would seek first is to decide if there is a novel the whole class will be reading in which a character has made good and bad decisions. The students can then either compare themselves (successes and failures) to the character, or they may write this paper from the character's point of view.

In science and social studies, this may become an evaluative essay. At mid-year, the students might write about the positives and negatives of their performance (focusing on the likes and dislikes in the content areas) thus far in the school year. In this case, the essay becomes more of a tool of self-evaluation for the student and the teacher.

Essays 1 and 2:

During your life, you have had both good and bad things happen to you. In these two essays, you will be describing these events. The organization of each essay is very similar.

Both essays must be five paragraphs with a 500 word minimum length. You must create interest in one essay with a humorous personal anecdote. In the other essay, interest must be created with a quote.

One essay will identify the best or three best things that have happened to you; the second essay will identify the worst or three worst things that have happened.

You may write either essay first, but you must write on both topics. I would very much like to see some humor or sarcasm in your best of times essay and want you to write the worst of times essay in an optimistic tone (what you learned from these events), rather than in a tone of self-pity.

Vocabulary for this unit:

inspirational	mesmerize	mar
indoctrinated	cynical	karma
optimism	pessimism	enthralled

ecstatic	overshadowed	peers
siblings	consequences	destiny
antagonize	jaded	minuscule
inferior	insubordinate	ego
ally	guru	flexible

| Charles Dickens | William Shakespeare | Ghandi |

To the victor go the spoils.
I've been down so long, it looks like up to me.

There Must Be Some Way Out of Here

My students have always enjoyed writing both of these essays. The topic is to describe what it would be like to be completely alone. At times, I have required students to bring items from home that they would want to take with them if they were to be alone (limiting this to a weight of five pounds). There have been some very humorous times with some of the most abrasive students bringing their cuddly stuffed animals and blankets.

For the self-contained teacher, the assignments can be restructured to allow students to place themselves into a historical setting in which there is a sense of hopelessness. In this case, the students are not alone per se, yet are "alone with their own thoughts."

They might, for example, imagine themselves as a young soldier before the first day of battle, a slave in either an ancient society or in early America, a homeless person in present society, or an investor during the stock market.

In science, a possible link might be to have students write about how it feels to be wrongfully accused while knowing they are right. Many scientists have had theories which proved to be true yet lived lives as outcasts or heretics until their theories were accepted.

Students understand their personal loneliness and frustrations. It is a very sensitive topic, and if presented in a way in which the students are inspired to write, their words can be remarkable.

Essay 1:

The two essays you will write this month are based upon a theme of being completely alone. Be creative and think of places where you could actually be alone — stranded on an island, in a lifeboat, in space, in the desert, in a cell, etc. These essays will link so be certain you choose a setting that will be interesting to you.

The first essay is a bit more of a short story to explain how you got to this place. It will not have a traditional opening paragraph but should start immediately with the story to create interest for the reader. Avoid using dialogue. I want you to write the story as if you are explaining it to someone after it had happened. I am looking for 500 to 800 words to effectively establish how you got into this predicament.

Essay 2:

This is a structured essay with an opening and closing paragraph and two, three, or four body paragraphs. You should create interest with a thought that keeps running through your mind as you analyze your situation. You might include a description of the setting, how you are surviving, what you might do to be rescued, what dangers are present in your environment, or what it feels like to know you are alone.

There are a number of things that cannot happen. You cannot meet any other people, you cannot die in the end, you cannot be rescued, you cannot discover a lifetime supply of food. You must live off of the environment. This essay should be at least 600 words.

Vocabulary for this unit:

isolated	impenetrable	aquatic
sustenance	bivouac	martyr
estuary	sustain	cliche
desalinization	circadian rhythm	stratify
precedent	subpoena	congenital
dysentery	forte	pagoda
unison	automation	pragmatic
mass media	silicon	phoenix
ethics	materialistic	microcosm

Robinson Crusoe   The Count of Monte Cristo

No man is an island

Take the easy way out

The End Is Near

This assignment can be written in a journal form, but you might consider using the paragraph structure as described below. The journal format will allow students the freedom to imagine that they were alive during a specific historical period and had to undergo a separation from the life they knew. They might still write about a time when a pet was taken from them, but they need to write the background in an historical setting. In other words, the emotions remain the same, but the setting can change to a different time.

The second essay is probably a bit too dramatic or disturbing to assign to third, fourth, or fifth graders as it is described below. It is thought-provoking, and you will find some very interesting classroom discussion will surface. Unfortunately, the idea can be tied into almost any period of history.

Essay 1:

At some point in our lives we all must leave something behind. We move to a new neighborhood, a friend moves on to another group or person, we outgrow a prized possession, or we have to give a pet away that is not allowed in a new apartment. We feel sad, disillusioned, and are certain that we will never get over the pain or frustration. In this essay, you will describe one of those times in your life when you had to leave something behind.

In your opening paragraph, you should describe your situation as it was prior to your finding out that a change was on the way. Your thesis will introduce the immediate thoughts that went through your mind when you were told the bad news.

Use two or three body paragraphs to describe the emotions you went through. Be careful that you do not repeat yourself in these paragraphs. Think about two or three different aspects of your emotions so that each body paragraph can focus a separate idea. Your closing paragraph should reflect your mood after you had accepted the change — it might be a day, a month, or a year later. You do not have to be happy about the change, just explain how you have coped with leaving something behind.

Essay 2:

You may have heard the expression "survival of the fittest." Basically, it means that the strong survive while the weak die. It was initially considered to be a description of the forces of nature. It also describes the plight of many humans over the course of history, but the definition might be reworded too: The politically strong survive, and the weak are the victims. This situation exists in several locations in the world today.

In this essay, you are to imagine that you are one of the weak and in constant fear of oppression, tyranny, or possible extinction by the strong. In the first paragraph, establish the setting. You may use one of the locations of the oppressed in today's society; we will discuss various situations in class.

Your body paragraphs should describe your feelings of fear, helplessness, hopelessness, and despair. Describe what you do to survive each day, what the effects are upon your family and friends, how you eat, how you sleep, how you get medical care. This should be written with a tone of desperation.

In the closing, provide some indication of why you are the oppressed, and why you do not or cannot join the other side. Is it a religious, political, spiritual, or intellectual commitment that will not allow to shift your views to save yourself? The catch is that you cannot decide to change sides. You need to describe why you will not do this.

Vocabulary for this unit:

equilibrium	maniacal	fervor
culminate	arid	initiative
perseverance	cultivate	intuition
leverage	self-talk	oppression
attribute	auditory	destiny
integral	caveat	evade

| introspective | aspirations | vanity |
| accomplishment | negligent | incessant |

| Viktor Frankl | Nelson Mandela | Hiroshima |

Ships that pass in the night.
Constantly looking over your shoulder.

A Character I've Never Known: Physical Description

If I were teaching in a self-contained classroom, I would link these essays to a novel we were reading in class or assign them as book reports. The first essay could be written having students describe a character who could fit into the story line of the book but does not actually exist in the book. In other words, the students would have to imagine and describe an entirely new character and fit him or her into the plot of the book. This is an excellent way to guarantee that the students have read the book and to assure that each of their papers will be unique.

The second essay could be assigned as though one of the book's characters were writing about the individual student. This sounds a bit confusing until you have read the description for the second essay. The setting for this essay might be one of the locales described in the novel. It is a rather strange approach, but it would certainly make reading these papers much more interesting than the typical book report.

Essay 1:

You will need to use your imagination to create a character in your mind. The character must be inspired by one of the stories you have heard in class. Your opening paragraph should relate an incident that the character experienced. The second paragraph should describe his or her physical appearance, the third, his or her personality. The closing paragraph should predict the character's future and close the essay.

Each body paragraph should be a minimum of 150 words, and the complete essay should have at least 600 words. I am looking for descriptive language. I want to be able to picture this character's expressions and style.

Please do not overuse the verbs: am, is, are, was, and were. Remember there are other linking verbs to substitute in their place.

Essay 2:

This essay uses a different approach in that you are going to imagine you are another person, and you will be describing yourself. To simplify the following explanation, you will be referred to as Person A, the person describing you is Person B. You must imagine you are actually Person B when you write this.

The opening paragraph should establish the setting. Be unique here. Place both Person A and B in an unusual location — a restaurant in a foreign country, a police station, a bus station, or in a courtroom — the choices are endless. Tell your first impressions when you see Person A enter the room.

In the body paragraphs, include a physical description, an analysis of Person A's gestures and style, and imagine what his or her personality might be.

In the closing, have Person A approach Person B and say a few words. Close your essay with a description of the Person A's voice and presence. There are some interesting twists that might be included in the final sentence.

Vocabulary for this unit:

maestro	prima donna	je ne se quoi
wanderlust	quintessential	stereotype
impresario	megalomania	inflection
clever	acquaintance	disheveled
incapable	disdain	tangent
generosity	caricature	indelible
debilitating	enervate	design
infatuate	freeloader	nonchalant

Charlie Chaplan	The Marlboro Man	Mark Twain

You can't judge a book by its cover.
Burn the candle at both ends.

Letter Writing: Two Different Approaches

It is a fairly obvious assumption that letter writing could be applied to almost any unit of study. Writing to a scientific or research corporation, writing to loved ones across the country in some historical setting, or corresponding with a fellow scientist or historian regarding a new discovery are three possible applications.

The second assignment is a bit more specialized and definitely has a late twentieth century theme. I do not have suggestions here about curriculum integration. I do know that it is a very humorous and challenging assignment for my students.

Essay 1:

At some point in your life, you will need to get a job. One of the best ways to impress a possible employer is to write a letter of introduction before you physically enter the establishment to fill out an application.

In this assignment you will write a letter requesting employment at a specific store or business. You must find the owner's name and address. Your letter must be typed, and you will continue to retype your letter until it is perfect.

Writing a letter is no different than writing an essay. In the first paragraph you must generate interest quickly (in one sentence), introduce yourself, and provide a brief thesis statement. The letter should be at least five paragraphs in length, but each paragraph will be fairly short and very specific. Busy people do not have time to read long letters.

Included in your body paragraphs should be the following information: your age, your unique abilities, how you will get to work, when you are available, what your parents think about your applying for a job, and why you want to work at that person's business.

The most important element is to convince the person why he or she should hire you. Why are you better than anyone else?

In the closing paragraph, give your phone number and tell when you are available to appear for an interview.

This is a business letter. Be certain you follow the guidelines for placing the inside address, greeting, salutation, and other formal letter components in their correct locations.

Essay 2:

This assignment involves another letter, but it will probably never be sent. It is fun to write if you choose a topic for which you have an interest and familiarity. A good topic is essential.

This letter will be written with a tone of sarcasm or understatement. One of the best ways to get a point across or to vent anger is to write a letter which is sarcastic or "tongue in cheek." There are some newspaper columnists who specialize in this approach, and I will read several samples in class.

Your paper should be a minimum of 400 words and at least four paragraphs in length. You must introduce your topic very clearly in the opening paragraph.

You need to let your creativity, humor, and imagination go on this one.

Vocabulary for this unit:

establishment	tenure	job market
employee	reference	hyperbole
understatement	pun	satire
cliché	environment	parody
instinctive	revenue	income
dramatic	subtle	overt
demonstrative	ironic	caustic
haphazard	mischief	riotous

Andy Rooney	Shel Silverstein	Dave Berry

Read between the lines.
Tongue in cheek

Biographical Sketch

The biographical sketch has an obvious link to any aspect of history or social studies. Writing this essay as though the person were a friend or acquaintance is the most interesting approach to use. The second essay can be assigned exactly as described below. Let the student create a scenario in which he or she was instrumental in causing the historical figure to make the correct decision. For example, the story, <u>Ben and Me</u>, is told from the point of view of a mouse adding to Ben Franklin's successes.

Essay 1:

Earlier this year, you wrote about yourself in an auto-biographical essay. Over the next two weeks, you will write a "biographical essay" or character sketch about someone you know well. You may not write about anyone who is a student at our school. You can write about a parent, a brother or sister, an aunt or uncle or any other relative, a family friend, a coach, or others who you find interesting. You must personally know the person. It cannot be a professional athlete or actor.

Your essay must be at least 600 words, and the opening paragraph must begin with an anecdote about the person. Your thesis should identify three or more aspects which are interesting about this individual, and you must have a body paragraph describing each of these aspects. The closing must link to the anecdote with which you began this essay. You must restate your thesis in a general way and provide a twist.

In your essay, explain why this person is interesting, why someone/anyone would like to know him or her, what impact this individual has had upon you and others, what makes this person unique, etc. Do not spend a lot of time with physical description. I am looking more for the personality and effect of this person's presence in your life.

Essay 2:

In the first essay, you described several events which, in your eyes, made the person interesting or unique. In this second essay, you must switch roles and now describe how your personality and friendship has influenced this individual to become the person you have described.

It may be that you will have to select a different person to describe in this assignment; however, even if you wrote about a close relative, your contributions to the relationship with this person have undoubtedly had an influence on his or her personality.

Create interest in the introductory paragraph by beginning in the middle of a story. For your body paragraphs, try to identify two or three of your personality traits or actions which have had an impact upon the individual. Close the essay with a link which completes or interprets the story you used to create interest.

This essay will take some pre-planning. Think about some clever ways in which you influence or affect others.

Vocabulary for this unit:

nom de plume	ethnicity	rebuttal
skepticism	confidant	advisor
alterego	conscience	reluctant
obtuse	consistent	amiable
frank	sociable	trustworthy
angst	fritter	bamboozle
irritating	egocentric	monger
indecisive	melodramatic	timid

Jiminy Cricket	Guardian Angel	Clark Kent

You can't see the forest for the trees.
Behind the scenes

Physical Disabilities: Blindness and Loss of Hearing

Essay 1:

Imagine what it would be like if for some reason you suddenly began to lose your vision. That is the topic of this essay. Over the next two weeks you will have some experience as to how this would feel. Your essay will be five paragraphs and between 600 and 800 words.

In the first paragraph, please describe how you became blind — what happened and how it happened. You

217

must use your imagination to create a realistic story. In class, we will discuss how blindness might occur.

The body paragraphs might present the simple things that you took for granted which are now impossible to do. For example, the dreams that you had that you will not be able to fulfill, the positive things that you have realized about being blind, or what it is like to know you will never again see faces and sights.

In the closing paragraph, be philosophical and optimistic. Explain to people what you have learned about sight and about being sightless. Give subtle advice and insight that you might think a blind person would actually provide.

Be careful to avoid preaching to the reader with lines like, "You should be grateful that..." or "You're just lucky that..."

Essay 2:

Loss of hearing might not be as devastating as the loss of eyesight, but it certainly would pose some new challenges. In this essay you are going to describe two scenes to a deaf reader based upon the image you hear in music. I will play three selections in class: "Also Sprach Zarathustra" by Strauss, "Allegro" (from the Four Seasons Suite) by Vivaldi, and "Flight of the Bumblebee" by Korsakov.

This is a four paragraph essay with the first paragraph explaining what you are attempting to do; that is, describe music (the scene created by music) to one who cannot hear it. The second and third paragraphs will be descriptions of two of the three musical pieces. The fourth will be a closing that allows you to imagine what it would be like to live in a world without sound.

Your essay should be about 600 words in length, and you must use vivid and precise vocabulary.

Vocabulary for this unit:

congenital	phobia	cataract
auditory	tactile	derogatory
visual	sensory	olfactory
retina	optics	distraction
self-serving	bifocals	obstruction
astigmatism	peripheral	keen
decibel	cochlea	disoriented
inaudible	disgruntled	pragmatic
Helen Keller	Anne Sullivan	Ray Charles

None are so blind as those who have eyes but will not see.
Beauty is in the eyes of the beholder.

Legends, Myths, Fables, and Tall Tales

At some point during the school year, your students are going to want to write with a bit more freedom than many of the essays described here. When students write legends, myths, fables, or tall tales, their imaginations take over. Regardless of the genre, these stories can link to the curriculum by having them explain some aspect of science that you have studied.

There are some interesting ideas which students might develop if this were used in conjunction with a unit on the human body. Instead of a natural phenomenon, you might ask students to create a legend as to "Why do people cough? hiccup? yawn? sleep? snore? cry?, etc." In the second essay, students would then have to evaluate and explain the scientific reason these occur. There are enough different and unusual physical actions that every student could write about a different idea.

The same approach could be used in almost any area of life science, earth science, or physical science.

Essay 1:

This is, perhaps, the most non-structured writing you will do this year. It is completely creative and allows you to let your imagination wander. Legends, myths, fables, and tall tales are specific genres of writing, but in this case, we are combining these concepts to have you explain, in a completely non-scientific way, why something is as it is. You need to imagine that you are an Indian medicine man or woman, a guru, a seer, a soothsayer, a shaman, a witch doctor, or another "uneducated" wise person who is responsible to explain things to your tribe or community.

Sample topics might be: Why the moon is silver/yellow. Why the sky is blue. Why bees buzz. Why there are stars in the sky. Why fish can breathe underwater. How the camel got its hump(s). Why the moon is full every twenty-eight days.

Since this is a story, there will be no "true" thesis statement. You should immediately begin your paper in the middle of the "action." Paragraphing should be done in natural breaks as the plot moves from one idea to the next.

Your essay should be approximately 650 words in length, and please avoid using sarcasm or cynicism.

Essay 2:

The second essay in this series is from the point of view of a skeptic; that is, a person who does not believe or accept what he hears. There are different types of skepticism. One type is based upon ignorance; for example, a member of a primitive society would not accept the fact the earth rotates around the sun based on the premise that he cannot feel any movement: therefore, the earth must be standing still. A second type of skepticism is based upon knowledge. In this case, one is a disbeliever because, based upon science and information, it seems illogical that a certain idea could possibly be true. For example, if a computer company advertised their new computer chip, claiming that it was physically impossible to create a chip that was faster than their new product, many would be skeptical of their advertising due to the rapid expansion of knowledge in the area of computer technology.

In this essay, you will use the latter definition of skepticism to develop a step-by-step rebuttal to a classmate's legend or fable. In other words, you will tear his or her story apart by using scientific fact to prove that the story cannot be true.

In this step-by-step process, you must write an opening paragraph which tells what you are going to do. Your body paragraphs should explain that point A is not possible because of this, point B is not possible because of this, and point C is impossible, etc. Your closing paragraph will present your opinion of how this natural phenomenon actually occurs.

You may assume the identity of a person within the village, a person living many years after the legend was first told, or you may be in the present day analyzing the validity of the tale. Explain your timing and position in the opening paragraph.

Vocabulary for this unit:

guru	soothsayer	shaman
observation	phenomenon	hut
element	occurrence	defer
orb	influx	climate
dismay	phosphorescent	reveal
despair	inevitable	reverberate
deceptive	skeptic	reality
conceal	denouement	demonic

Aesop   Mother Goose   Will Rogers

Last but not least
Proof positive

Supporting an Opinion

These assignments might be given as a book report or
to have students debate some aspect of history. Expressing
one's opinion could obviously be used with almost any social studies or science unit.

Essay 1:

This assignment is a bit on the strange side (not a
completely unusual situation). You will choose three
words that are your favorites. They may be meaningful,
humorous, pointless, motivating, etc. You will then write
a five paragraph essay — opening, three body paragraphs
(one per word), and closing.

Your opening paragraph should create interest by using
a famous quote or lyric. You should then interpret the
quote to the point that it leads into your thesis, in which you
introduce your three words.

Your body paragraphs should give a clear description
as to why a particular word is so meaningful to you. The
best way to do this is to tell a short anecdote which explains
how this word came to be interesting.

Your closing should link to the quote. Perhaps you might provide a different interpretation of the quote than that which you offered in the opening. Then you must restate and twist.

I am looking for clever explanations here. Do not use phrases like, "I like this word because..." or, "This is one of my favorite words because...." Do not even think of using a word which has a double (off-color) meaning or is in any way inappropriate.

Essay 2:

In most speeches, the speaker has one purpose in mind; that is, to convince you that his or her way is best. In this essay you will write a speech in which you will persuade your classmates why your opinion about some controversial topic is correct. It should be structured similarly to any other essay. You must gain the listener's interest, provide convincing arguments for your side, and end with a clever closing that your audience will not easily forget.

Vocabulary for this unit:

assumption	expression	accomplice
fait accompli	diversion	debate
clarity	precision	disclaimer
interpret	decipher	decode
expressive	irrelevant	detractor

retaliate	so-called	tongue-tied
gabby	monotonous	cheeky
obscure	wishy-washy	divulge

| Miriam Webster | Daniel Webster | Roget |

No one wins an argument.

There's no time like the present.

One Step at a Time

These essays are good practice if your students are going to do a science project. The methodical, step-by-step approach is easy to teach to younger children and demonstrates very clearly that each paragraph has a specific purpose. There are limitless possibilities in having students write a description of a historical event or to explain a scientific phenomenon.

Essay 1:

This essay is a step-by-step explanation of how to do something. You need an opening paragraph to convince the reader why he or she would want to learn to do this. The body of your essay should have at least five steps (five paragraphs).

Some sample topics might include: How to shoot a free throw. How to complete an essay. How to borrow money from your parents. How to train a dog to sit. How to ask a boy or girl to dance. You need to tell the reader how to choose proper equipment, how to get organized, and how to accomplish the task.

Your closing paragraph should again remind the reader of why he or she should do this and reinforce the great feeling of accomplishment achieved for completing the task.

Essay 2:

This assignment is like a "Dear Abby" advice column in that you will pose a problem and give a step-by-step method of resolving the situation. The extra ingredient is that you must be one who both presents the problem and provides the solution.

Your question should be one paragraph in length and clearly spell out a problem that will take two, three, or four steps to resolve. You need to give sufficient information so the reader fully understands your predicament.

In your answer, sympathize with the author in the first paragraph, respond with the steps in the body paragraphs, and close the essay with words of optimism and support. Your complete paper should be at least 400 words.

Vocabulary for this unit:

altercation	dilemma	previous
successive	plethora	terminate
echelon	dichotomy	disregard

predicament	claimant	obstacle
ongoing	conscience	trait
reaction	obsessed	inclement
sabotage	underlying	superficial

Ann Landers   Poor Richard   Dear Abby

Mind your P's and Q's.
The proof is in the pudding.

Decisions, Decisions, Decisions

Essay 1:

At some point in our lives we all have to make a difficult decision or choice. As much as we want to participate in two activities, sometimes we simply have to choose one over the other. This is the topic of your essay.

This should not be written about a decision which was a matter of right and wrong. I do not want you to unveil a dark secret about something you have done. You need to do some thinking about your topic before you start writing.

The suggested format for the essay is six paragraphs. You should have opening and closing paragraphs plus four body paragraphs. In the body, explain choice one, choice two, what you decided and why, and the ultimate effect. You need not follow this exact structure, but it should be of a similar format and length (minimum 500 words).

Essay 2:

We are all born with certain inherent qualities or abilities. Some have beauty, some have intelligence, some have musical talent while still others are humorous or insightful. What would it be like if we could select our best attributes rather than inheriting them?

In this essay, you must decide whether you would choose to be beautiful (handsome), intelligent, or popular. You cannot be all three; in fact, in this essay you can be "the most" in only one category, you can be average in a second, and you are "the least" in the third. For example, you may choose to be the most popular in school and have average looks, but you are the least intelligent in your class.

In three body paragraphs (one discussing each attribute), explain why you made your choices and support your decisions with examples.

The opening paragraph should use a biographical incident to create interest.

Vocabulary for this unit:

characteristic	attribute	ability
idealism	catharsis	ignorance
sophistication	peers	dilemma
inconsequential	plethora	tension
unleash	deception	accelerate
detached	focal point	I.Q.

| mensa | converse | adjacent |
| ethereal | gregarious | invalid |

| The shell game | Fairy Godmother | Saint Peter |

Pay the piper.
Take it with a grain of salt.

What is it?

These assignments would be considered persuasive if categorized into one of the domains of writing. For a self-contained teacher, the essays will link to any aspect of history in which people were being persuaded or brain-washed into a specific action. For example, free land in the West, opposing a dictator, religious freedom in another land, volunteering for military duty, or signing one's name on a document of protest. To convince countrymen to follow a particular path, a sales pitch or persuasive argument had to be presented.

In the area of science, the same type of application might apply in convincing peers that certain aspects of scientific research are acceptable. For example, research performed on laboratory animals, test groups using a new medication, cloning of a new or perfect species, or the cost of space exploration. Students would not typically see these as a sales pitch, but that is precisely what they are.

229

Essay 1:

This is a five paragraph essay in which you will create a sales pitch for a new product that is "essential" for everyone. I will give you a sample of the product, and you have to create its purpose, its development, its name, its importance to society, and why everyone must have one (many).

Write an opening paragraph to interest the reader in the product. Your three body paragraphs will identify different important features of this amazing new invention. The closing will make that final pitch as to the importance of owning this product.

Essay 2:

Many times after we have been convinced that a product is worth buying, we find that the commercial was misleading or greatly exaggerated. Think of a time in your life when you wanted a particular item very badly, but once you purchased it, it quickly broke, was lost, or did not perform up to your expectations.

Write a four or five paragraph essay in which you tell the saga of this purchase. The opening paragraph should talk about the excitement of anticipating the purchase, the body paragraphs should describe the various things that went wrong, and the closing should summarize what you learned from this situation.

Subtle humor and understatement would be a nice addition to this essay. Try to explain the circumstances without exaggerating; instead, write the essay with a "straight face." I will explain more about this concept in class.

Vocabulary for this unit:

icon	invaluable	appliance
intriguing	apparition	essential
devious	enervated	obsessive
maladjusted	provocative	excessive
shill	discerning	calculating
dishonest	inflated	measly
incapable	objective	con man
obnoxious	generous	trinket
Zig Ziglar	P.T. Barnum	Carney

Never give a sucker an even break.
There's another sucker born every minute.

Song Essay

There are very few students who do not love music. While we may not necessarily embrace the music our students listen to, I have found writing about music is highly motivational. I remind my students that the song they choose for this assignment may not contain any inappropriate language or innuendo (this seems to limit the choices more and more each year).

Linking this to other curricular areas is difficult at best, so in this case, this becomes writing for writing's sake. It is an assignment which most of my students have enjoyed.

Essay:

In this assignment, you have an opportunity to be more creative in the organization of your writing. Because songs differ so greatly, it would be impossible to limit your writing to one format. Select one of the following ideas and use it as a basis for your essay.

Idea 1: Identify one, two, or three possible interpretations of the lyric and write a four (or five) paragraph essay using the standard structure.

Idea 2: Tell how the music and lyric work together to complement one another.

Idea 3: Create a story based upon the theme or people in the song. This will not follow a traditional essay approach. I will discuss this in class.

Idea 4: Select a character or characters in the song and write a description of him, her, or them. Use your imagination. Include more than just a physical description and include personality and background information. Create a complete character.

Idea 5: Tell why you like or dislike this song and support your opinion with three reasons one way or the other. Do not do both in the same essay.

Science Project

The science project has been a staple of writing programs for many years. Here are my thoughts as to how this assignment might be presented.

Cover Page: Title of project, name, class period, date, teacher's name.

Hypothesis: Write it as though you are writing an opening paragraph. You must create interest as well as present your thesis. Your point of view must be first person.

Example

We all know that what the nose is able to smell and what the mouth is able to taste are somewhat the same. I was wondering, if the other senses (sight, touch, and hearing) were completely eliminated and the remaining two senses were directly compared, which would be more sensitive, taste or smell. It is no easy task to eliminate sight, touch and sound completely, but I suppose that if I can do this, then I could simply have someone taste a flavor while holding the nose or smell an aroma while covering the mouth. I believe that given this situation, the sense of smell will prove to be more efficient in identifying flavors than the sense of taste.

Research: Writing your research section in first person is a challenge; it does, however, make it almost impossible to copy directly from any source. That is why you must write your paper in this format.

You have to imagine that you are giving a lecture on your topic, and you are the authority. Everything that is important to know about the topic was discovered by you and therefore, "I" can be used throughout. I have included a sample from a science project from several years ago.

The research paper should be at least three pages typed (not including drawings or clip art), double spaced with no bigger than a 12 point font. Fewer than three pages will cost you a lot of points and more than five pages will gain no extra points.

Example

A "sense" can be defined as any of the body's functions which allow a person to take in information from the outside world. I can feel hot and cold, I can taste food or poison, I can smell fragrances, I can hear a million different sounds, and I can see colors, shapes and objects. My senses are the only way for me to know what is going on outside of my body! Now most people believe that we have only five senses but other scientists and I now believe that we may have as many as twelve or thirteen senses. For example, I can sense the passage of time, and I can sense when someone is near me without the use of my five "basic senses." Some people can read minds (or so they say), and most of us can "sense" danger. Regardless of how many senses I have or some mystical guru in India claims to have, my experiment focuses on the five basic senses and how they work.

Taste is probably my favorite sense. There is very little that can top the taste of hot sausage pizza, perfectly buttered popcorn, an ice cold Pepsi, or a Papa John's chili dog! Have you ever wondered why these things taste better than brussel sprouts or broccoli? It all has to do with the taste receptors on our tongues.

Basically we can only perceive four tastes — sweetness, sourness, saltiness, and bitterness.

Materials: I want a very specific list of materials needed, the size of the servings, the reason you chose what you chose, how you are going to time it, how you are going to record data, etc.

Procedure: In several short paragraphs I want to know the step-by-step procedure of how you are going to do (how you did) your experiment and recorded your data. I want this detailed enough so that I can replicate your exact process and materials.

If you are using Bandini Whole Grow Rose Fertilizer to plant your plants, and you purchased it at Green Thumb Nursery, I want to know that as well as the size of the bag and how much it cost.

If you planted flowers in green plastic pots that are two inches by two inches by four inches and have four holes in the bottom, I want to know that. I want to know where you purchased them. If you are going to ask seven questions to your volunteer subjects, I want to know the exact, word-for-word questions in the same order that you asked them.

If you use a Maytag Model 3417 washing machine on warm water cycle for permanent press fabrics and added one-half cup of Clorox bleach after the rinse cycle, I want to know not only that, but I want to know if it was powder or liquid bleach. I think you get the picture.

Results: Again, specifics count. Exactly what did you learn. Were there any exceptions? Were there any irregularities? When precisely did you do the test? How might the results have been different under different circumstances (if that applies)?

The presentation of these sample assignments is a starting point. There are no two teachers who teach alike. Please use what you like, change the structure to fit your grade level, or recombine them into different sets. I cannot guarantee they will work for you; however, I have shared these ideas with many teachers, and I know they are working very well for them.

Shortcuts in Correcting

I have yet to do a teacher workshop when a question has not surfaced regarding the amount of time it takes to correct an extended writing assignment. To put this into perspective, I have seventy-five students in my three eighth grade writing classes (I also teach three sections of Spanish). Each student writes a 500 to 1000 word essay every two weeks for a total of sixteen essays. In addition, students write two in-class essays of approximately the same length. Each year, I correct approximately 1350 essays. Needless to say, I do a lot of correcting.

In the writing plan which I propose for elementary and secondary teachers, the correcting load becomes similar to mine. If a teacher is to make a commitment to work this hard to improve the writing of students, we need to look at some of the simple logistics and time involved. We then need to use every technique possible to shorten the amount of time spent on each paper.

If I were to allow an average of 30 minutes to correct each paper, it would take 675 hours per year! In a 180 day school year, this would mean three hours and forty-five minutes of correcting each school day. By correcting papers on Saturdays and Sundays, I could reduce my correcting time approximately two and one-half hours per day. This does not include planning, meetings, conferences, or tutoring. My reaction — forget it! We cannot afford to spend thirty minutes on each essay.

If I spend ten minutes per extended paper, correcting will take 225 hours per year. In 180 days that works out to an hour and fifteen minutes per day. If I correct on Saturdays and Sundays, this shrinks to about fifty minutes per day. Given the amount of time I save in planning by organizing my writing program into two related assignments per month, vocabulary tied into writing, homework assignments becoming somewhat generic with an ongoing assignment, and the benefit in having students do so much writing, I can live with fifty minutes per day of correcting.

Elementary teachers may be thinking, "But I have to correct math papers, reading work, etc." Let us take a look at the reality of your situation. With thirty students in class, if each individual writes an extended paper every two weeks (sixteen per year), you will collect 480 papers in the course of the year. If each paper takes ten minutes, eighty hours will be spent correcting. This breaks down to less than thirty minutes per day, five days per week, or twenty minutes per day if you correct on Saturday and Sunday.

Again, given the amount of prep time saved in preparing sets of writing assignments; vocabulary lessons; integration of literature, science, and social studies; universal homework, and application of spelling, grammar, punctuation, usage, computer, and handwriting; twenty minutes of writing assignment correction per day is a very workable commitment. Now we face the challenge — correct a thousand word essay in ten minutes? How?

We need not identify every mistake a student makes in a writing assignment. If we are going to read as quickly as we must, some errors are going to slip by. Using the ten techniques described in this chapter, and blending these ideas with the time-saving techniques you have already developed, I believe it is possible for every teacher to adhere to a ten minute time frame per paper.

Use a Timer

The timer I use is a 60 minute ticking timer which I purchased for $4.00 at a local hardware store. Mine ticks out loud, and I love that sound. If the ticking annoys you, buy a digital timer.

When you begin correcting the first paper in that stack of thirty, seventy-five, or one hundred and twenty papers, set the timer to ten minutes. Monitor yourself and make conscious decisions that if five minutes have passed and you are still making comments on the first paragraph, you are working too slowly. Forget about being perfect and start being realistic.

239

Once you get the feel for a ten minute span of time, set the timer for thirty minutes. Force yourself to correct three papers during this time.

We do not yet have all the specific shortcuts to attain this magical ten minute goal; more ideas are forthcoming. Your first step is to get a timer so you can begin to measure your progress.

When the timer is ticking, do not allow yourself to be interrupted. Lock your door, do not answer your phone, hide from those who would peer in through your windows, and spend the ticking time focused upon the paper at hand.

Do not over-correct

When was the last time that you received relentless criticism? Do you ever want to return to that place or to visit that person? When we over-correct a paper, that is precisely what we are doing to a student.

When does criticism work? We can accept criticism when is constructive; that is, when our errors are pointed out with specifics, and when we are given suggestions as to how we can gain the approval of the superior who has made the criticism.

If the boss says, we are not doing a good job, and we need to work harder, we become resentful. We question what is good enough to satisfy our employer.

If the boss says we are not doing a good job because the work we do is messy or incomplete, but then adds, "Here are two samples of the quality that I am seeking.

Notice how the examples clearly delineate the step-by-step process. Each step is numbered and each identifies two or three checks to be certain you are headed in the right direction."

When we receive this type of directed criticism, we can control our situation without guessing. While we may feel insecure about our performance, we know precisely how we can make immediate improvement. When we correct a student's paper, we must keep this in mind.

In any extended essay, a student will make a variety of errors. I always correct for mechanics — spelling, usage, punctuation, and capitalization, but I also keep the ten minute timer in mind. If a students has made twenty or so mistakes in the opening paragraph, there no point in meticulously correcting the next two, three, or more paragraphs. It is at this point that I decide what specifics I can ask this student to address on a rewrite or on the next paper. Generally, I will try to find two positives and two specific points to work on.

Example

You did a nice job of introducing the topic, and I like many of the words you have chosen. They paint a clear picture of the scene. Two areas which need work are the sentence structure and neatness. The first paragraph is eleven lines long, but you only have two sentences. You need to read your paper aloud and decide where the natural pauses occur. On your next paper, I do not want to see any sentence longer than eight words. I also believe you can write more neatly. Take time and take pride in the work you hand in. There are many good points in this paper, but better sentence structure and neatness would make it much better.

This is a rather long note to students, but it is typical of the type of note I write on each paper. It takes me about three minutes to write this much, but my students and the parents of my students are very appreciative. They ignore the fact that I may have missed a misspelled word here or there. They realize that there is a specific area in which they can improve. This is the most important aspect of correcting a paper.

Use numbered rules to simplify correcting

In the chapter on punctuation, a list of comma rules are presented. If you use these rules when correcting papers, you need not take time to write the student a note about how to apply a rule. Simply write in the correct punctuation with the rule number above it. If an unnecessary comma is used, write a question mark or WR? (what rule?) above the comma.

The alternative here is to write in the comma without explanation. When a teacher does this, he or she has become an editor, and no learning or teaching is taking place.

Handing a paper to a student with a series of ③'s written above missing commas, focuses him or her on a specific skill which can improve writing and the grade. You will be amazed how quickly you can correct for commas (and semicolons) using this technique. A numbering approach can be used for capitalization rules as well (+5, -3, etc.). A sample set of numbers is presented in the chapter on capitalization.

Make clear correcting labels for repetitive comments

Several years ago I was correcting papers and became frustrated at having to write the same comment on one paper after another. I had some clear mail return address labels, and a brainstorm hit. I typed a series of comments on the computer (see next page), formatted them to fit on the clear labels, and started affixing them to students' papers rather than taking the time to write. Because the labels are clear, I can place them directly over the students' errors. They can read my comment and still see their writing through the label.

Creating the first label sheet was very time consuming (at least two hours), but now I duplicate four or five copies on labels each time I have a set of papers to correct. I am convinced that with each assignment, I save at least two to three minutes per paper by using labels rather than having to write comments. That may not seem significant, but over the course of a year, three minutes per paper saves over seventy hours. The initial two-hour investment is well worth it.

Use a rubric to keep correcting consistent

I usually avoid the word "rubric" simply because it has become such an educational buzzword. Since teachers seem to understand a "rubric," it makes more sense to use that term. I prefer to call it the "writing checklist."

This page is a 50% reduction of the original size.

Column 1

Comma Rule 1
Use a COMMA after an introductory word,
phrase, or clause.
Yes, I believe so
In the past, I was...

Comma Rule 1
Use a COMMA after an introductory word,
phrase, or clause.
Yes, I believe so
In the past, I was...

Comma Rule 1
Use a COMMA after an introductory word,
phrase, or clause.
Yes, I believe so
In the past, I was...

Comma Rule 1
Use a COMMA after an introductory word,
phrase, or clause.
Yes, I believe so
In the past, I was...

Comma Rule 1
Use a COMMA after an introductory word,
phrase, or clause.
Yes, I believe so
In the past, I was...

Comma Rule 2
Use a COMMA between two descriptive
adjectives that can be flip-flopped.
The loud, obnoxious dog
The light brown dog (no COMMA)

Comma Rule 2
Use a COMMA between two descriptive
adjectives that can be flip-flopped.
The loud, obnoxious dog
The light brown dog (no COMMA)

Comma Rule 2
Use a COMMA between two descriptive
adjectives that can be flip-flopped.
The loud, obnoxious dog
The light brown dog (no COMMA)

Comma Rule 3
Use a COMMA between three or more items in
a series – COMMA before "and" is optional
Jim, Randy and Rene
Jim, Randy and Rene

Comma Rule 3
Use a COMMA between three or more items in
a series – COMMA before "and" is optional
Jim, Randy and Rene
Jim, Randy and Rene

Comma Rule 4
Use a COMMA between two complete sentences
joined by and, but, or, nor, for, yet
He went to the party, and he was late
He went to the party, and he was late (no COMMA)

Comma Rule 4
Use a COMMA between two complete sentences
joined by and, but, or, nor, for, yet
He went to the party, and he was late
He went to the party, and he was late (no COMMA)

Comma Rule 4
Use a COMMA between two complete sentences
joined by and, but, or, nor, for, yet
He went to the party, and he was late
He went to the party, and he was late (no COMMA)

Comma Rule 5
Use a COMMA to offset unnecessary or
parenthetical phrases or appositives.
She, to be sure, was surprised

Comma Rule 5
Use a COMMA to offset unnecessary or
parenthetical phrases or appositives.
She, to be sure, was surprised

Comma Rule 9
Use a COMMA to begin and end quotations
unless you use a I or ?
"I hope," she said, "you will join me."
"Why not?" he asked

Comma Rule 9
Use a COMMA to begin and end quotations
unless you use a I or ?
"I hope," she said, "you will join me."
"Why not?" he asked

Comma Rule 7
Use a COMMA between dates and years
May 10, 1999

Comma Rule 8
Use a COMMA between cities and states but
not between states and zipcodes
Solvang, CA 93463

Column 2

Comma Rule 1
Use a COMMA after an introductory word,
phrase, or clause.
Yes, I believe so
In the past, I was...

Comma Rule 2
Use a COMMA between two descriptive
adjectives that can be flip-flopped.
The loud, obnoxious dog
The light brown dog (no COMMA)

Its - it's
It's means it is (ONLY!) Think of the apostrophe
as the missing I
Its is a possessive (ownership)
It's too late to fix its broken leg.

Its - it's
It's means it is (ONLY!) Think of the apostrophe
as the missing I
Its is a possessive (ownership)
It's too late to fix its broken leg.

Its - it's
It's means it is (ONLY!) Think of the apostrophe
as the missing I
Its is a possessive (ownership)
It's too late to fix its broken leg.

Its - it's
It's means it is (ONLY!) Think of the apostrophe
as the missing I
Its is a possessive (ownership)
It's too late to fix its broken leg.

loose - lose
loose means not tight (rhymes with noose)
lose means unable to find
His shoes were loose, and he was afraid he
would lose one of them

NOMINATIVE CASE PRONOUN
I, you, he, she, it, we, they, who
always put yourself second – he and I

NOMINATIVE CASE PRONOUN
I, you, he, she, it, we, they, who
always put yourself second – he and I

choose - chose
choose means to select (rhymes with shoes)
chose is past tense of select
Today I choose the same shoes that I chose
yesterday

choose - chose
choose means to select (rhymes with shoes)
chose is past tense of select
Today I choose the same shoes that I chose
yesterday

who's - whose
who's means who is (ONLY!)
whose is a possessive (ownership)
Who's the person whose voice is loud?

who's - whose
who's means who is (ONLY!)
whose is a possessive (ownership)
Who's the person whose voice is loud?

If the owner is singular, add 's after the word
(Bob's books)
If the owner is plural and ends in s, add '
(boys' books)
If the owner is plural and doesn't end in s, add 's
(women's books)

If the owner is singular, add 's after the word
(Bob's books)
If the owner is plural and ends in s, add '
(boys' books)
If the owner is plural and doesn't end in s, add 's
(women's books)

**Don't end one sentence and
begin the next sentence with the
same word or phrase.**

**Don't end one sentence and
begin the next sentence with the
same word or phrase.**

**There are no such words as
alright and alot**
Always write
all right and a lot

**There are no such words as
alright and alot**
Always write
all right and a lot

**Don't begin two consecutive
sentences with the same word
or words.**

Column 3

**Don't repeat a highly descriptive
word in the same paragraph.**

**Don't repeat a highly descriptive
word in the same paragraph.**

**Don't repeat a highly descriptive
word in the same paragraph.**

already - all ready
already means previously
all ready means completely prepared
He had already made certain they
were all ready

"I" comes before "e" except after "c" or when
sounded as "a" as in "neighbor and weigh
Exceptions: in leisure seize neither nor their
weird, foreign ancient height either and don't
forfeit counterfeit protein or caffeine

"I" comes before "e" except after "c" or when
sounded as "a" as in "neighbor and weigh
Exceptions: in leisure seize neither nor their
weird, foreign ancient height either and don't
forfeit counterfeit protein or caffeine

brake - break
brake means to stop a car
break means destroy or ruin
If the brake doesn't work, I'll break my neck

brake - break
brake means to stop a car
break means destroy or ruin
If the brake doesn't work, I'll break my neck

past - passed
past is noun or preposition meaning "by"
passed is a past tense verb telling an action
In the past I have passed past the door

past - passed
past is noun or preposition meaning "by"
passed is a past tense verb telling an action
In the past I have passed past the door

quiet - quite - quit
quiet means without sound
quite means or extremely
quit means to stop working
It was quite quiet in the office when I quit

quiet - quite - quit
quiet means without sound
quite means or extremely
quit means to stop working
It was quite quiet in the office when I quit

than - then
than is a comparison
then tells when
It'd rather go then than now

than - then
than is a comparison
then tells when
It'd rather go then than now

than - then
than is a comparison
then tells when
It'd rather go then than now

too - to - two
too means more or less than necessary or "also"
to means toward (say 'uh' to decide)
two is more than one

too - to - two
too means more or less than necessary or "also"
to means toward (say 'uh' to decide)
two is more than one

there - their
there is a place (here) or the beginning of a
sentence or independent clause
their shows ownership (e-i-e-i-o)
There are students at their desks over there

there - their
there is a place (here) or the beginning of a
sentence or independent clause
their shows ownership (e-i-e-i-o)
There are students at their desks over there

Column 4

threw - through
threw is past tens of throw or toss
through tells where (a preposition)
He threw the ball through the tire.

threw - through
threw is past tens of throw or toss
through tells where (a preposition)
He threw the ball through the tire.

weather - whether
weather is the conditions outside
whether is a choice (whether or not)
The bad weather will help us decide whether or
not to go.

weather - whether
weather is the conditions outside
whether is a choice (whether or not)
The bad weather will help us decide whether or
not to go.

weather - whether
weather is the conditions outside
whether is a choice (whether or not)
The bad weather will help us decide whether or
not to go.

**Avoid beginning every sentence
with a pure subject. Use ...**
examples: Since, while, Due to, in addition to,
according to, one may also, even though,
although

**Avoid beginning every sentence
with a pure subject. Use ...**
examples: Since, while, Due to, in addition to,
according to, one may also, even though,
although

Avoid overused words:
examples: fun, like, boxed, boring, nice,
really, good, supposed to,

Avoid overused words:
examples: fun, like, boxed, boring, nice,
really, good, supposed to,

Avoid overused words:
examples: fun, like, boxed, boring, nice,
really, good, supposed to,

Capitalization
Don't capitalize words like high school,
circus, school, or club unless it would be
written on a sign in front of the building

Capitalization
Don't capitalize words like high school,
circus, school, or club unless it would be
written on a sign in front of the building

**Don't end one sentence and
begin the next sentence with the
same word or phrase.**

**Don't end one sentence and
begin the next sentence with the
same word or phrase.**

**Don't end one sentence and
begin the next sentence with the
same word or phrase.**

**Don't begin two consecutive
sentences with the same word
or words.**

**Don't begin two consecutive
sentences with the same word
or words.**

**Don't begin two consecutive
sentences with the same word
or words.**

One question I often ask when I meet with a group of teachers is, "What is the difference between an 87 and 93 on a paper?" The response in many cases is, "My mood." When we correct a paper on Friday night and are tired, or that student had a bad day in class, his or her score might be an 87. By the same token, on Saturday morning, when we are fresh and have had a chance to forget about the previous day, the same paper might garner a 93. We must be honest. Grading a writing assignment is subjective, and the grade we give is often a reflection of our mood.

A teacher can minimize this fluctuation by using a rubric (shown below). When I first began using this method, I typed the evaluation criteria on a separate sheet of paper and then stapled it to the student's assignment.

I found I could type an abbreviated version of each criteria item on a 1" by 4" white mail label and affix it directly in the margin of a student's paper. This saved shuffling an extra sheet of paper and also amazed my students with the cleverness of this idea.

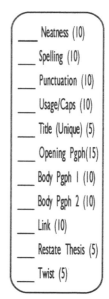

____ Neatness (10)

____ Spelling (10)

____ Punctuation (10)

____ Usage/Caps (10)

____ Title (Unique) (5)

____ Opening Pgph(15)

____ Body Pgph 1 (10)

____ Body Pgph 2 (10)

____ Link (10)

____ Restate Thesis (5)

____ Twist (5)

When an assignment is given, the criteria by which it will be graded is shared with the students. This is in keeping with my philosophy of providing specifics for students. This criteria, in a very abbreviated form, appears on the label. I find by using this method, my grading, whether Friday night, Saturday morning, or Tuesday after school, remains very consistent.

What I particularly like about providing a rubric is that each students can identify specifically why the grade is as it is. Two students may receive a score of 78; however, one of them may have been cleverly written but contains numerous points subtracted for mechanics while the second student may have wonderful mechanics but very poor explanation and creativity. The writing checklist focuses each student on what needs improvement.

The rubric might be different for each assignment. The first example is typically what I would use for the first few months of the school year. There is a heavy emphasis on mechanics. My goal is to let students know specifically if their spelling, punctuation, usage, or capitalization is a problem.

The second example is more typical of what I use beginning the third or fourth month of the school year. Note that all mechanics combine into one category and more points are given for the content and creativity of the writing.

_____ Neatness (10)
_____ Mechanics (25)
_____ Opening paragraph - interest/thesis (10)
_____ Body Paragraphs - one topic/multi-senses (30)
_____ Closing - link/restate/twist (10)
_____ Creative Approach (15)

By the fourth quarter, I simplify the label even more. By this time of the year, I know individual student's strengths and weaknesses very well, and my focus is getting all students to attain the level of the goal paper.

Type your comments

Many teachers type very quickly and many write very illegibly. You may find that when you have finished reading a student's paper, the fastest or neatest way to provide the lengthy feedback described above is to type your comments on a 2" by 4" label and then affix this to the student's paper.

If you decide to use this method, set up a template on the computer that shows the imaginary lines of the label edges. This is an easy task on any newer computer.

When writing lengthy comments, I have a tendency to get a bit messy because I am trying to write so fast. When you type your comments, they are always legible. You can use spell check to catch any embarrassing errors you might make.

Do not type one comment and print the label. Wait until you have corrected ten papers (ten labels per page) and print the entire sheet. Be certain to type the student's name on each label.

This approach can be taken a few steps further if you like playing with computer gadgetry and new technology. There are several voice recognition programs on the market. These programs allow the user to talk while the computer translates your voice into written text.

If it sounds too good to be true, at the start, it is. I use a voice recognition program, and after much practice, it is only about 90% accurate. I have to reread and make corrections. It is currently a much longer process to talk than to type. I am confident, however, that if I keep at it, and the computer learns my voice, this method will enable me to correct papers faster.

A second technology trick which you might consider is to program your handwriting to a computer font. This is no small feat, but once it is accomplished, you can actually type and see your own handwriting unfold on the computer screen. When I type comments to students and print them on labels, they are in my own handwriting! I can even change the size of the font to fit more onto a 2" by 4" label. Several of the computer draw or drafting programs provide instructions on how to do this. There are other computer programs specifically designed to perform this task. It takes some time to create your own font, but the results are amazing.

Nibble at writing assignments

It can be overwhelming to receive a stack of thirty essays on a Friday morning. We look at a two or three inch pile of papers and realize how much work it will be to get these back to students. For the junior or senior high school English teacher, that stack of papers can be eight to twelve inches high.

If we are determined to correct writing assignments for thirty to sixty minutes per day, we will read three to six papers. I play a game with myself, trying to correct another three or four papers during the school day.

Before students enter the classroom in the morning, correct a paper; before getting a cup of coffee at recess or going to eat lunch, correct one; during your prep, correct one; and when students leave at the end of the day, correct one. Nibbling away at a stack of essays is a surprisingly effective technique. You will be amazed that the ten minutes spent here and there is time you will never miss. You still have time for breaks and lunch, but that overwhelming stack of papers will begin to shrink.

Stress neatness on every paper

The rubric or writing checklist previously described includes ten possible points for neatness on every assignment. Each paper we receive that is sloppy, wrinkled, or illegible takes more time to correct. It is not our job to decipher the scratchings of lazy students, and if we accept this responsibility, more of our students will become lazy.

On the first extended writing your students hand in, be very strict on the ten points for neatness. I often give zero points or one point in this category when a paper is difficult to read. Students will sometimes complain, "But I don't have nice handwriting." True, some students handwriting is less appealing, but any student can take the time to form letters correctly, indent, write a name on a paper, avoid drawing in the margins, write in ink (if required), turn in an unwrinkled paper, and center the title. If we do not have this expectation, who will?

If poor quality continues, I begin to deduct points for spelling anytime a word is written illegibly. Students will again complain, "But I spelled it correctly, look." My response is, "I could not read it!"

249

Some students are physically incapable of writing in a legible manner (each year I have a student or two who fall into this category). When this occurs, set up a meeting with the student and parent and begin the discussion that this student may need to type his or her paper.

As teachers, I believe we must take a realistic approach to what these students will be doing five or ten years from now. If a student cannot spell or cannot write legibly, then he or she must learn alternatives to overcome this disability — type, use spell check, have classmates help with proofreading, use a dictation machine, or hire a transcriber.

We must help the student and the parents find a solution, but we cannot allow a student to use this as a lifelong crutch. An employer or a college does not care. Teachers care, but we must take the approach of, "Deal with it."

Neatness is essential on a job application, a letter of introduction, or simply writing a check. We need to stress this skill as early as possible.

Avoid numerous rewrites

The decision as to when enough is enough is a challenge. We want students to see what a final, corrected copy looks and feels like. When we make comments on a draft, it is nice to see how a student implements our suggestions. Unfortunately, if our students always do a rewrite or final draft of a writing assignment, our correcting time has almost doubled. This is too much of an obligation.

There are two basic reasons why we must limit the number of opportunities a student has to rewrite an assignment. First, we have to do that much more correcting; second, students will figure out that they can do a poor job on the first attempt, and we will become their editors. Their rewrites will be excellent, and they will not have applied themselves.

Teachers have a variety of ways to assure that students have done pre-writing and editing before completing their final draft. Many teachers collect the rough draft and final draft together. Some teachers correct the rough draft before requiring a final draft. Some simply collect the final draft.

I fall into the latter category. My eighth graders do their rough drafts paragraph by paragraph over a week or two. We spend fifteen to thirty minutes per day reading aloud, discussing, and answering questions. I put samples on the board, give advice on how to accomplish the specific goals of that particular assignment, and answer individual questions students have after class or during my prep. Sometimes, if a student is having a particularly difficult time, I will keep his or her paper and record comments (see next section) for pick up later that day. I try to avoid this.

When my students hand in their finished essay, it is a final draft. I correct it, grade it, and return it with suggestions focusing on the next assignment. Depending upon the group of students, there are times I select three essays during the year which every student must rewrite. I never let them know if they will have this opportunity. Another approach I have used is that any student whose grade is a 75 or lower must do a rewrite.

One suggestion to consider: If your students do a rewrite, grade the rough draft and grade the final draft but average the two grades together. For example, if a student merely goes through the motions on the rough draft (to force you be the editor) and is graded only on the final draft, receiving an 85, what has been taught? If, on the other hand, the same student receives a 44 on the rough draft and an 85 on the final, the average score is 65. A subtle message has been sent.

Younger students — fourth through sixth graders — need to be taught the process of revising and editing prior to writing a final draft. Even with younger students, be careful about taking on the responsibility of correcting their rough drafts for them.

The process of reading paragraphs aloud each day, doing models in class, and providing practice on specific skills is much more effective teaching than collecting a set of papers, correcting, and returning them to students.

Have students write at home and read at school

In the chapters on year-long planning and the monthly homework assignment, a process is suggested to have students work on their writing assignments paragraph by paragraph, night by night.

My students do very little work on their extended writing assignments in class. They write at home, and we read samples in class. The writing in class is on sample paragraphs, linking paragraphs, and practice.

The easiest day I could have in class is to give students thirty minutes to write. If I do this, I pay the price after school by having to correct sets of papers. I prefer to spend my time in the front of the classroom, teaching. The interchange between a student reading a sample and my comments are invaluable to the whole class. If you restructure your classroom to operate in this manner, you will be amazed at how you can lighten your correcting load.

Use a cassette recorder

One of the most efficient methods to get information to students is to record your comments rather than writing them. I use a small cassette tape recorder with a built-in microphone and speakers.

I started using tapes many years ago when one or two of my students wrote papers which were almost unintelligible. It would have taken a twenty minute meeting with the student to provide all the necessary feedback to even get them to "ground" level. Most of what I would have said would have gone right over the student's head anyway. There is only so much that any of us can remember when something is being explained verbally.

It dawned on me that recording the comments would allow students to listen to the tape several times and would also eliminate the need to sit down one-to-one with the student. In a departmentalized setting, it is almost impossible to find students or to pull them from other classes when *you* have time to meet. The tape solved this problem.

On a tape, a teacher can, in five minutes, say what would take twenty minutes to write. One caveat when using tapes — force yourself to be positive. Find anything on which to compliment the student because most of what you have to communicate is negative. A tape is a permanent copy so be aware that parents or others may listen.

Correcting papers will never rank high on a teacher's "love to do" list, but it is a requirement of the job. Using the techniques described above will make the task manageable.

One reality we must keep in mind is that when we add something new to our teaching responsibilities, something else must be dropped. These are conscious decisions we must make. The decision to have your students write (and you correct) more writing than they have ever done before mandates that something else in your curriculum be curtailed or eliminated.

It is obvious that I believe extensive writing ranks evenly with reading and math as the focal point of the curriculum. Teaching writing is the most difficult, yet is also the most satisfying, of all subjects. I improve every year as a writing teacher. I hope the suggestions provided in this text will enable you to move to a new level in teaching your students to write.